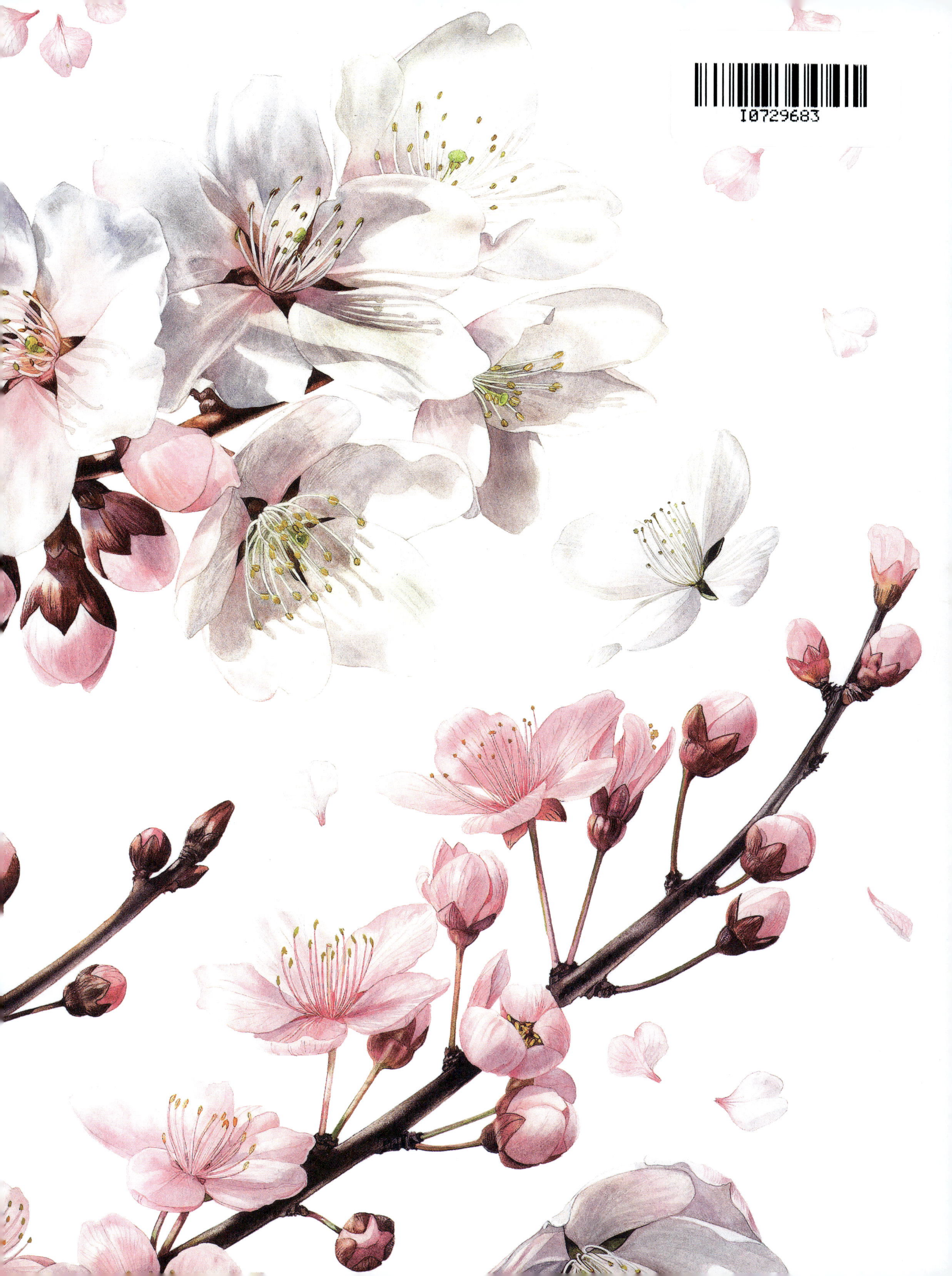
I0729683

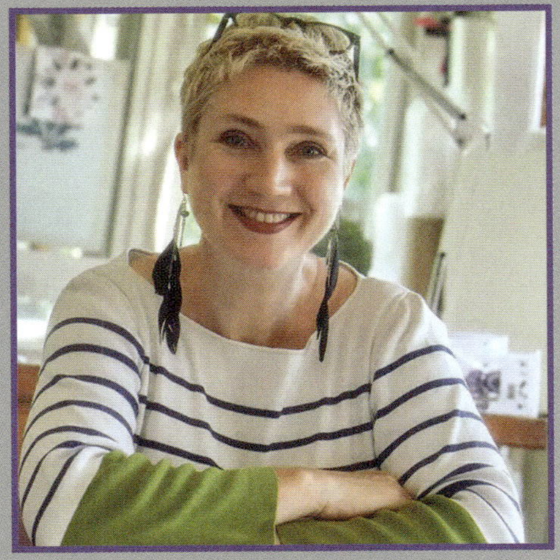

BILLY SHOWELL is an internationally
renowned botanical painter, illustrator
and tutor and is based in Kent in the
UK. Her works are distinguishable by
her striking compositions, and she has
won several botanical awards as well as
selling over 48,500 copies of her books
to date.
Billy's work is held in the collections
of the Royal Botanic Gardens, Kew,
the Hunt Institute (USA) and in the
Shirley Sherwood Collection as well as
in private collections worldwide.
Visit her website: www.billyshowell.com
and her Instagram: @billy_showell

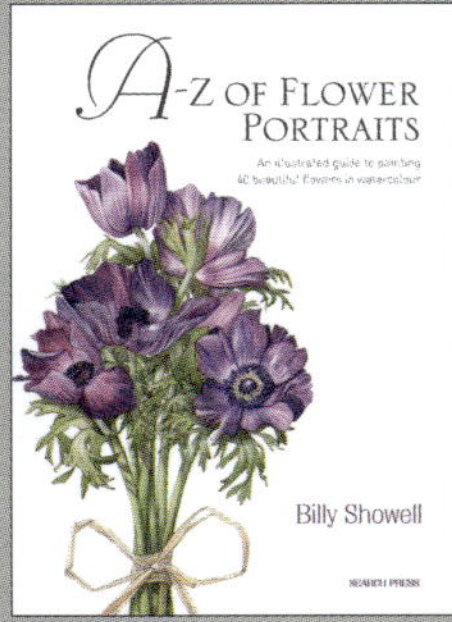

978-1-84448-452-2

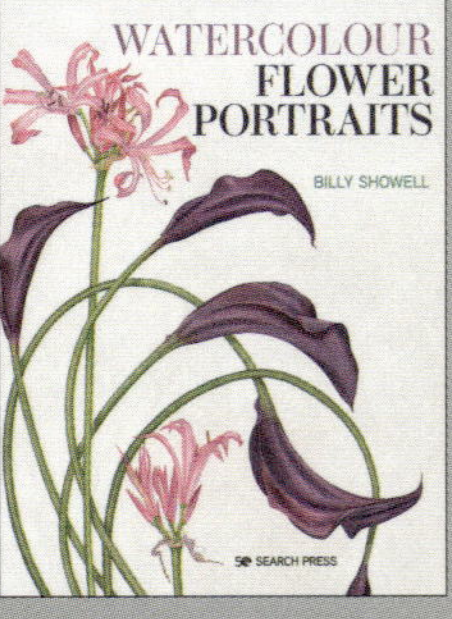

978-1-78221-961-3

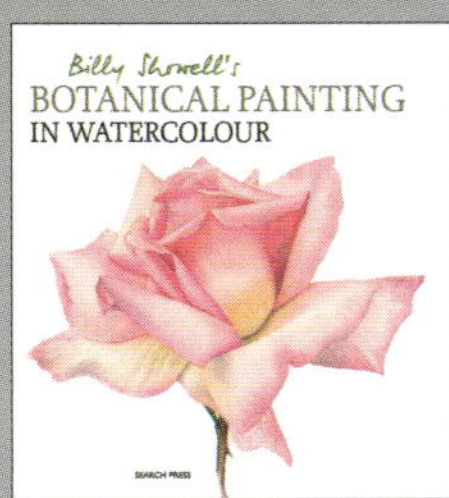

978-1-84448-451-5

The BOTANICAL SHOES

BILLY SHOWELL

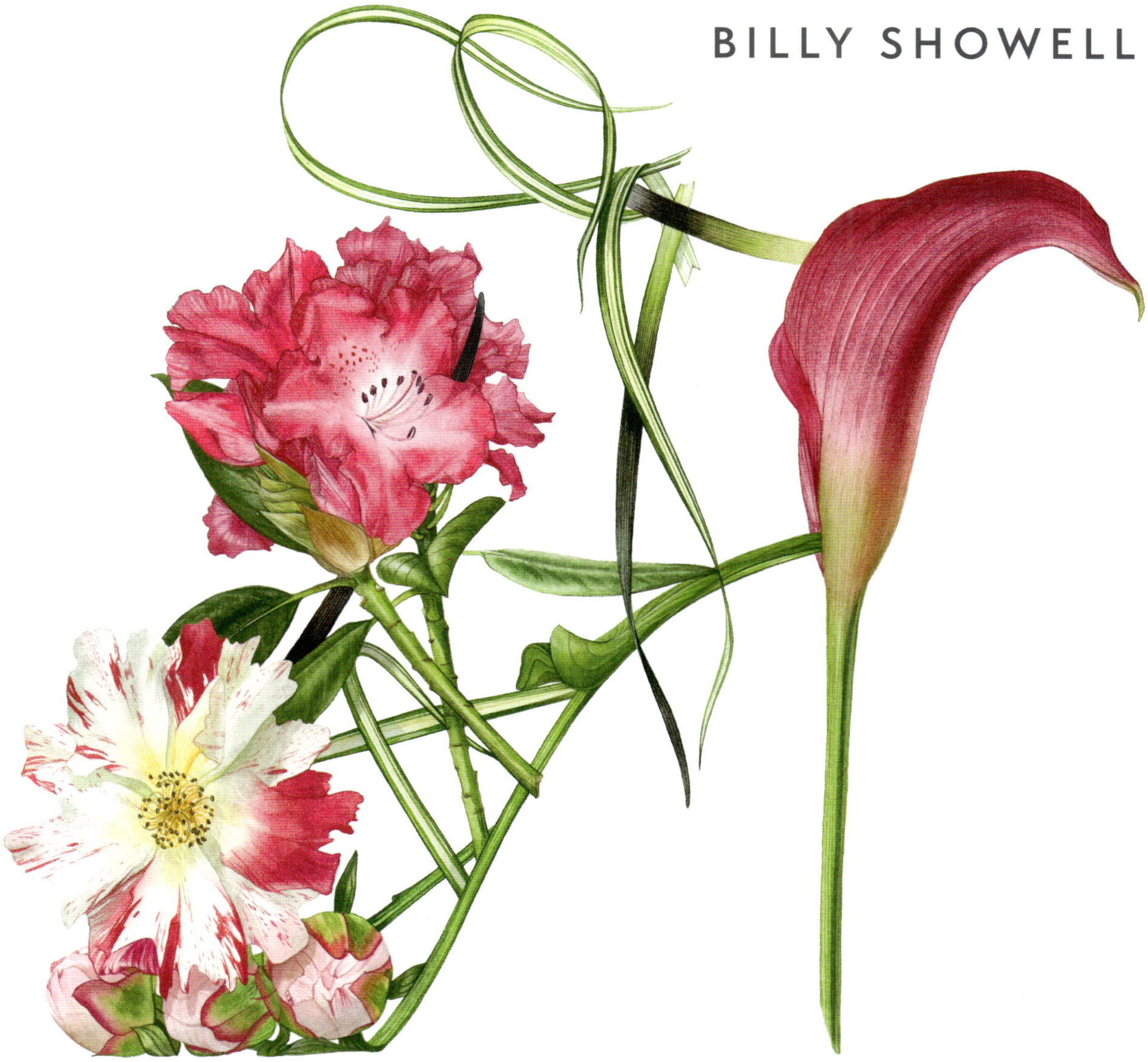

A COLLECTION OF BOTANICAL SHOE PAINTINGS
IN WATERCOLOUR

SEARCH PRESS

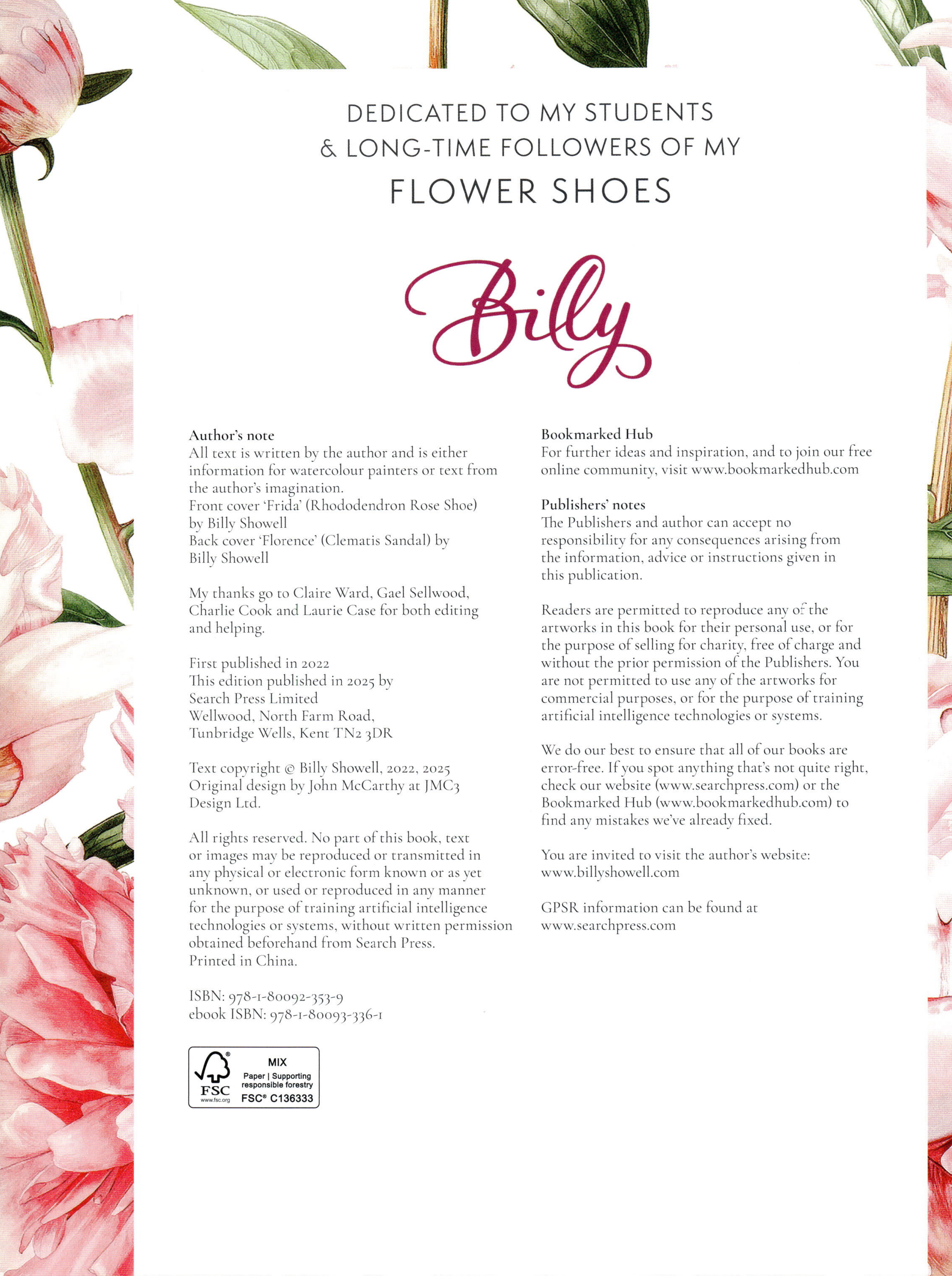

DEDICATED TO MY STUDENTS
& LONG-TIME FOLLOWERS OF MY
# FLOWER SHOES

Billy

Author's note
All text is written by the author and is either
information for watercolour painters or text from
the author's imagination.
Front cover 'Frida' (Rhododendron Rose Shoe)
by Billy Showell
Back cover 'Florence' (Clematis Sandal) by
Billy Showell

My thanks go to Claire Ward, Gael Sellwood,
Charlie Cook and Laurie Case for both editing
and helping.

First published in 2022
This edition published in 2025 by
Search Press Limited
Wellwood, North Farm Road,
Tunbridge Wells, Kent TN2 3DR

Text copyright © Billy Showell, 2022, 2025
Original design by John McCarthy at JMC3
Design Ltd.

ISBN: 978-1-80092-353-9
ebook ISBN: 978-1-80093-336-1

Bookmarked Hub
For further ideas and inspiration, and to join our free
online community, visit www.bookmarkedhub.com

Publishers' notes
The Publishers and author can accept no
responsibility for any consequences arising from
the information, advice or instructions given in
this publication.

We do our best to ensure that all of our books are
error-free. If you spot anything that's not quite right,
check our website (www.searchpress.com) or the
Bookmarked Hub (www.bookmarkedhub.com) to
find any mistakes we've already fixed.

You are invited to visit the author's website:
www.billyshowell.com

GPSR information can be found at
www.searchpress.com

CONTENTS

My heritage	4	BLUE LILAC	64
Flowers	6	Blue lilacs	66
The first shoe	9		
Gathering	10	BLUE	74
My tools	13	Blues	76
How I design	14		
		PURPLE BLACK	80
THE BOTANICAL SHOES		Purple blacks	84
and the fantasy	16		
Love colour	20	GREEN	92
		Greens	92
CREAM YELLOW	20		
Cream yellows	20	Reflection	97
RED	34	The shoes, paintings	
Reds	36	and their plants in	
		order of appearance	100
PINK	50		
Pinks	52		

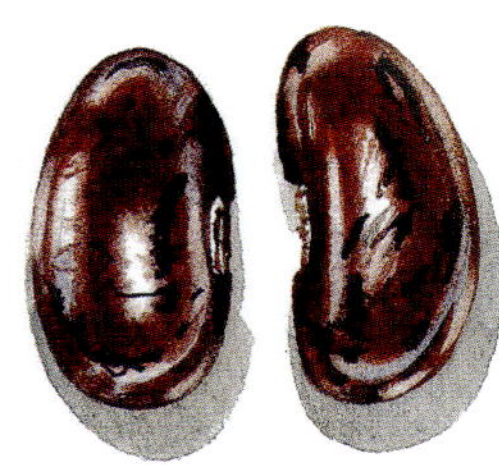

MY HERITAGE

My father's pencils lay alongside mine, with two seeds from his runner bean collection. I painted these to remember both the growing of the beans and my mother's famous runner bean chutney.

I inherited Dad's love of painting and Mum's love of home-making, and I honour all that they taught me. My father was an artist and calligrapher. He bestowed in me the love of perfecting one's art with the joy of 'the line', the happy swish and glide of a confident brush, and the glorious rush of a perfectly simple composition. I will always be grateful for these gifts and many others they bestowed upon me.

HOPE

I do believe there is a place somewhere, where we can find
a life at peace, in

happiness.

Maybe we find it on the path that we call life.
Maybe we will never rest upon it as a destiny.
Perhaps we find it in the thoughts or actions of others or indeed ourselves.
We might not recognize it in the moment.
It might take all the time we have to find it,
and only then see it through clouded eyes.
Some may seek it in creativity,
Some in planting seeds.

We may know it only for an instant.
And of course, we may not know it when it is found.
But seek it we will.
A life in peace and happiness.
Perhaps it is never truly known
but woven discreetly into the love we receive,
and the love we give to others along our way.

I find joy and peace in painting, and studying plants,
delighting in their structure and colour.

My past is adorned with the plants I grew up knowing; their scent drifts
and carries me along the floral pathways of my memory.

TRAVEL

I travel through life backwards
Never seeing what's to come,
I plant for the succeeding gardener,
And cherish the green on my thumb.

If I turn to see what's ahead
I'll miss cherishing what's gone before,
So, I will water my roots and nourish my mind,
And let my creativity soar.

I travel through life backwards
never seeing what is to come.
I'm never prepared,
I'm always surprised,
And cherish the green on my thumb.

FLOWERS

My mother's garden was always awash with peonies, roses and azaleas. She would plant and tend them gently and their blossoms would saturate our spring and summer seasons. So, to me, a home is only home when the flowers make it so.

This is my inheritance from my mother.

Some may call it shadow
A cast to steal the light.
Some will call it shade
A summer's day delight.
My shadow is my gift to you
my shadow is a pool,
of calm where you can find the space
and place to keep you cool.

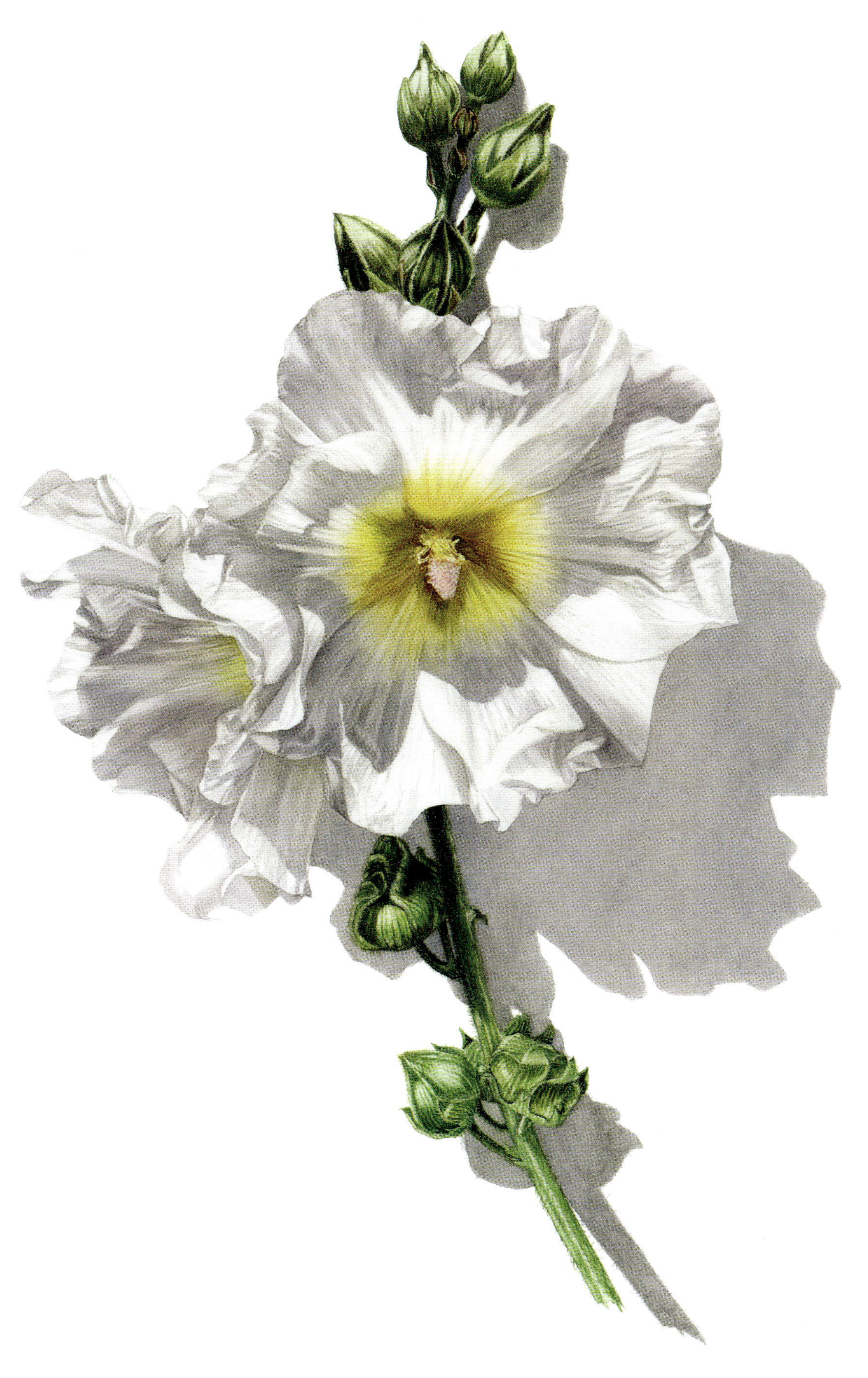

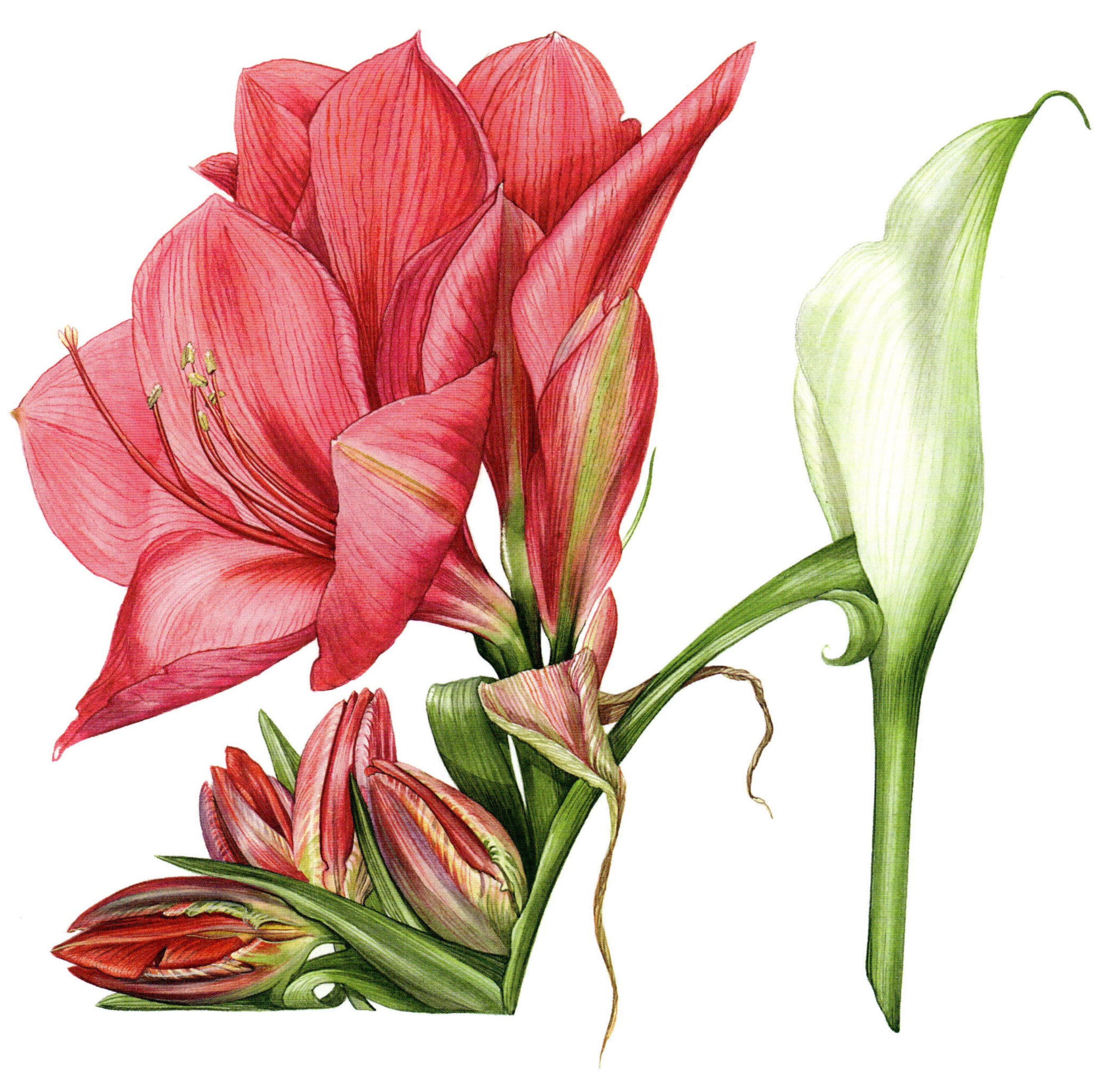

THE FIRST SHOE

The shoes began through a happy mistake,
a flower painted in an awkward place.

As I endeavoured to find a way of saving the painting from abandonment, I stepped back and only then began to see the possible heel of a shoe. The lily was still too far left, but with the subtle placement of a bud to represent the toe, and a gentle curve of a leaf connecting them, a shoe silhouette appeared on the paper.

Excited, I set about creating another shoe silhouette to make a pair. Boots followed, and yet more shoes after that. Each design informed the next. There were endless variations, some obvious and some subtle.

What was entrancing was the distinct fragility of the shoes: imaginary shoes, shoes that can never be worn. There is a delight in composing something new every time.

It is an escape from the mundane, the obvious, and the well-trodden. It is an opportunity to dream.

I am now revealing to you the main collection as it stands today (although there are a few shoe paintings that have skipped their way to family and friends and escaped capture).

This book is a gathering of flowers, a celebration of nature's colours and a step into fantasy.

The words I have chosen to accompany them hint of journeys, perhaps to find love, home or belonging. Only now and then do I gently interrupt the dreams with what I hope are helpful painting notes.

Discover which shoes you would choose; where, I wonder, where would they take you?

GATHERING

Gather flowers in the morning
still lambent with dew,
greet them warmly as you pick,
and say thank you as you do.

Choose the view that calls to you,
a view speaks about the bloom.
Place its feet in a flower vial,
and keep it cool to keep its style.

Gathering cut flowers in the morning ensures they retain optimum moisture.
The night air has kept them cool and their stems are rich with food and moisture.
Immediately place them in a deep-water vase until you are ready to paint them.

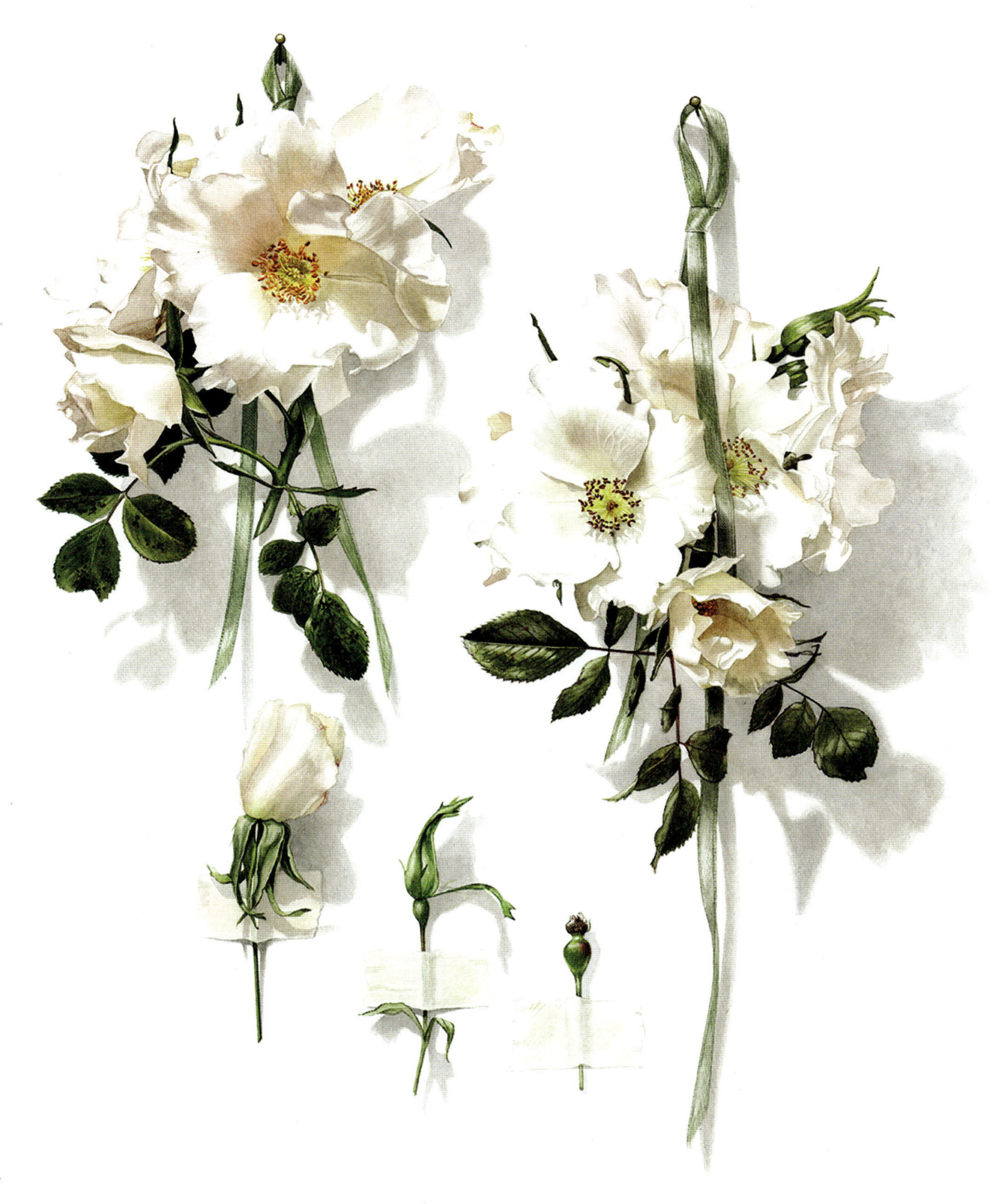

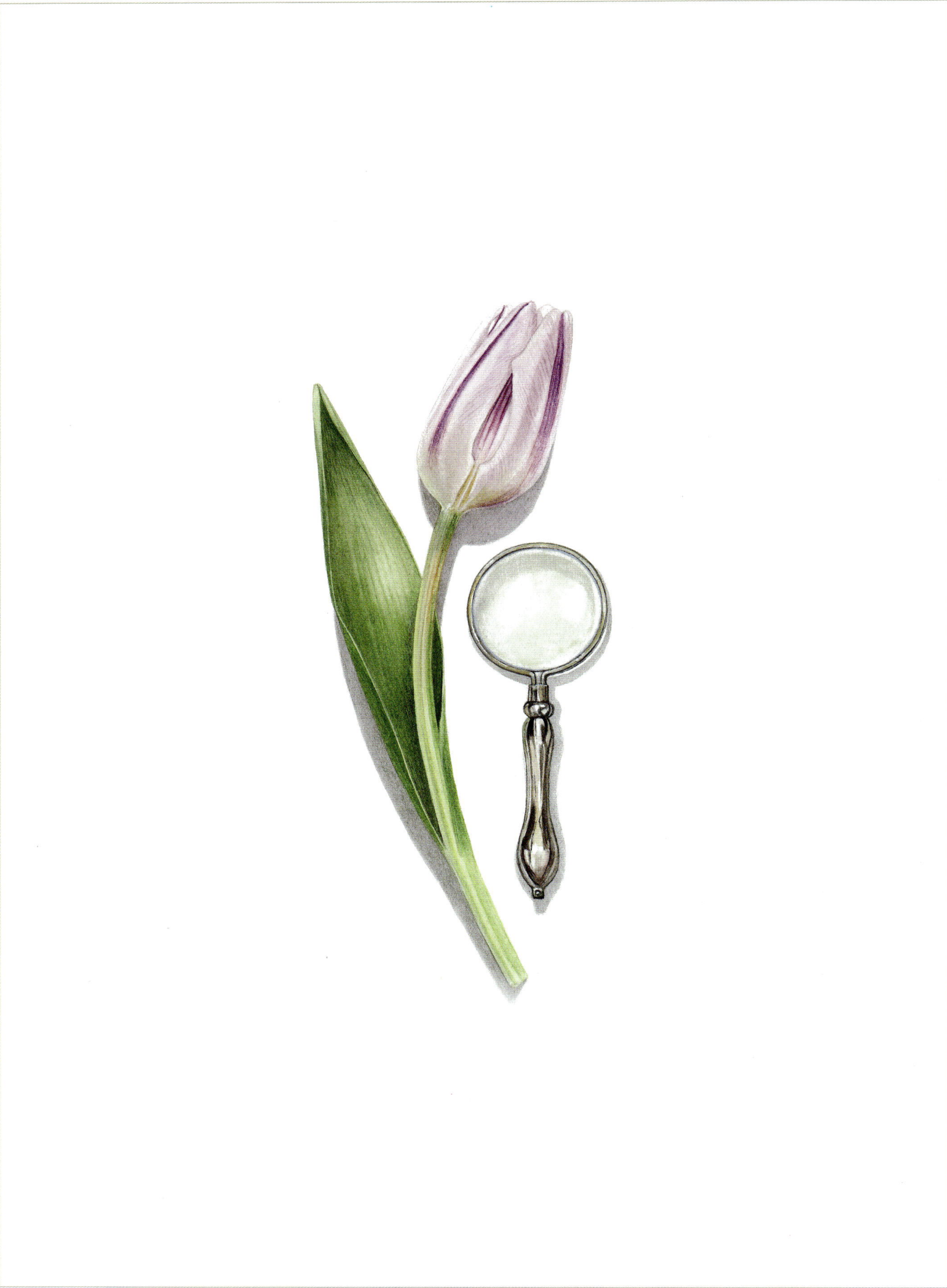

MY TOOLS

I have chosen my tools,
packed them carefully into my case,
And taken delight in their order.
I hurry away to a pool of shade
to paint the wild flower border.

In reality, my shoemaking tools are my gardening equipment, paints, paper and brushes.

Here, I have hinted at a world where we are at one with nature and have no need for shoes, and if we did, they would only need to be made from the delicate plants we come across.

The shoes are noetic, a concept or an idea to describe the fragility of plant life, a dream of how we might be in tune with and more tender towards nature. Indeed, I try to work with homegrown flowers and plants from bulb or seed or cutting, or from the place that I have found them growing.

You will have seen that there are QR portals in this book which will take you to my website, where I show you how to paint my way. If the fantasy footwear inspires you to paint, you can see how they were created and perhaps paint along with me. On my site, I share all the information you might need to start painting flowers or fruits and vegetables, and what you need in order to improve your observation of detail and colour through the medium of watercolour. Sharing my painting tips and techniques has been a delight and pleasure throughout my working life.

I now choose to use synthetic brushes, sizes 6, 4, 2 and 1, as they have long-lasting properties and great resilience. I also use my eradicator brush. Years ago, when I first started to teach, I introduced the 'eradicator' to my students. It was my invented name for an unassuming, small chisel brush that was soft enough not to damage the paper but strong enough to erase mistakes; my students would laugh at the name and often call it 'The Terminator' by mistake.

My eradicator brush is also useful for creating texture and perfecting edges. I use my Divine wash brush for larger painted areas and my sturdy mixing brush for the freedom to mix paint without having to damage my other brushes. Last but not least, I have a fine liner, a tiny slim brush that is great for little areas and dry brushing. I predominantly use 100 per cent cotton hot-pressed paper, as it is strong and takes the layers of paint beautifully.

I still use the same small art case from the first day that I set out travelling with my paints.

I adore collecting plants, painting tools and small objects to inspire me, and I often paint in a 'collection style' form of composition. I find comfort in collections of things, repetition and order, and perhaps creative comfort in a less-expected arrangement.

I love to paint images of my creative tools; it is a way to pay homage to the dexterity of the craftsmen that made the tools and to those that use them in their craft. I like to paint in detail, study the intricacies of natural forms, revel in 'the small', and paint pretty, perfect, portraits of plants. Through what I paint, I am focused and yet not too serious. I find small adventures in the compositions that fall from the tip of my paint brush, I follow to see where they will go. I think the shoe paintings fulfil the desire to make a collection of less-expected compositions.

HOW I DESIGN

The design will start with the plant, and then, as the artist Paul Klee suggests ('A line is a dot that went for a walk'), I begin to take the pencil for a walk, or, as I prefer to think of it, a dance.

I sketch straight onto my painting paper, light and loose. For my shoe paintings, I aim to conjure the structure of a shoe and try to imagine it being worn. The heel is often the starting point, and the shoe will grow from there and flourish. Long stems are often chosen to weave it together and add straps to the design.

I prefer fresh flowers to work from as the shadows are softer and the colours more accurate. This is especially true with the leaves; I need to curve and twist them to help me construct the required shapes.

Each shoe is an exercise in composing and selecting the flowers to complement each other. One must find the right way to create the shapes without compromising the plants. Once you tune into the elements that go into any design, you start to see them in the flowerbed. I find myself buying plants for the garden with paintings already in mind. Grasses and leaf shapes are essential tools, as they increase the essence of fragility and add an element that ties the flowers together.

For me, this evokes a memory of stitching and assembling shapes to make garments. Making and designing clothes has been a love of mine ever since I could thread a needle. How things connect and feel as you are making them, and understanding how shapes knit together to create volume, is a constant fascination of mine.

Through painting the shoes, slippers, and boots, I can fashion them in two dimensions from the beauty found in nature.

Sometimes I will arrange the fresh flowers into a design. This is rare, as one has to work very fast, but the process of doing this is truly delightful. One really gets to know the plant and how it catches the light from different angles. I often think of myself as a painting flower arranger.

Finally, I will stand the painting on the far side of a room to see it from a distance and contemplate whether it is finished. I can return to a picture over several seasons, waiting for the right plant to appear to complete the design.

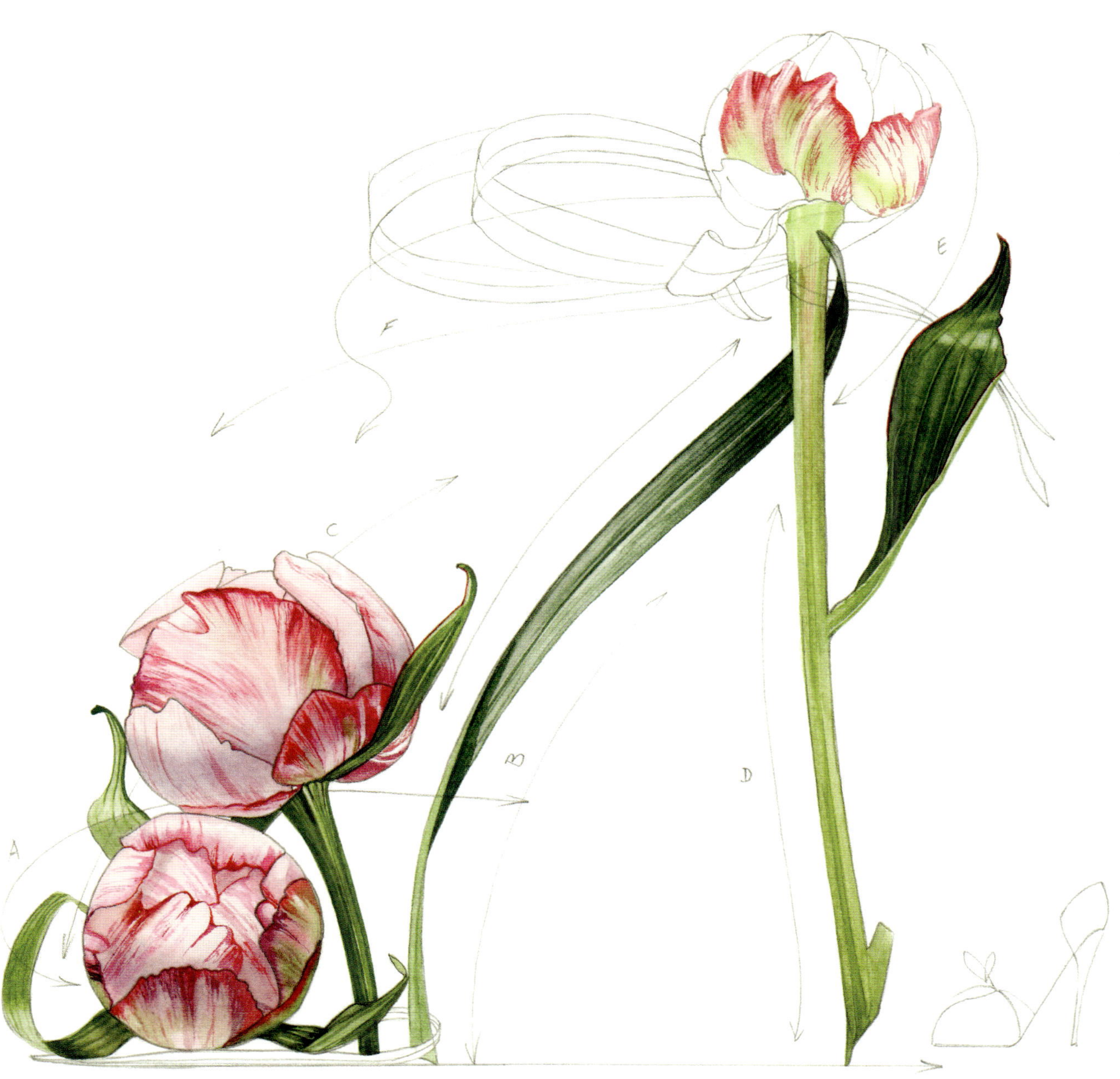
A
B
C
D
E
F

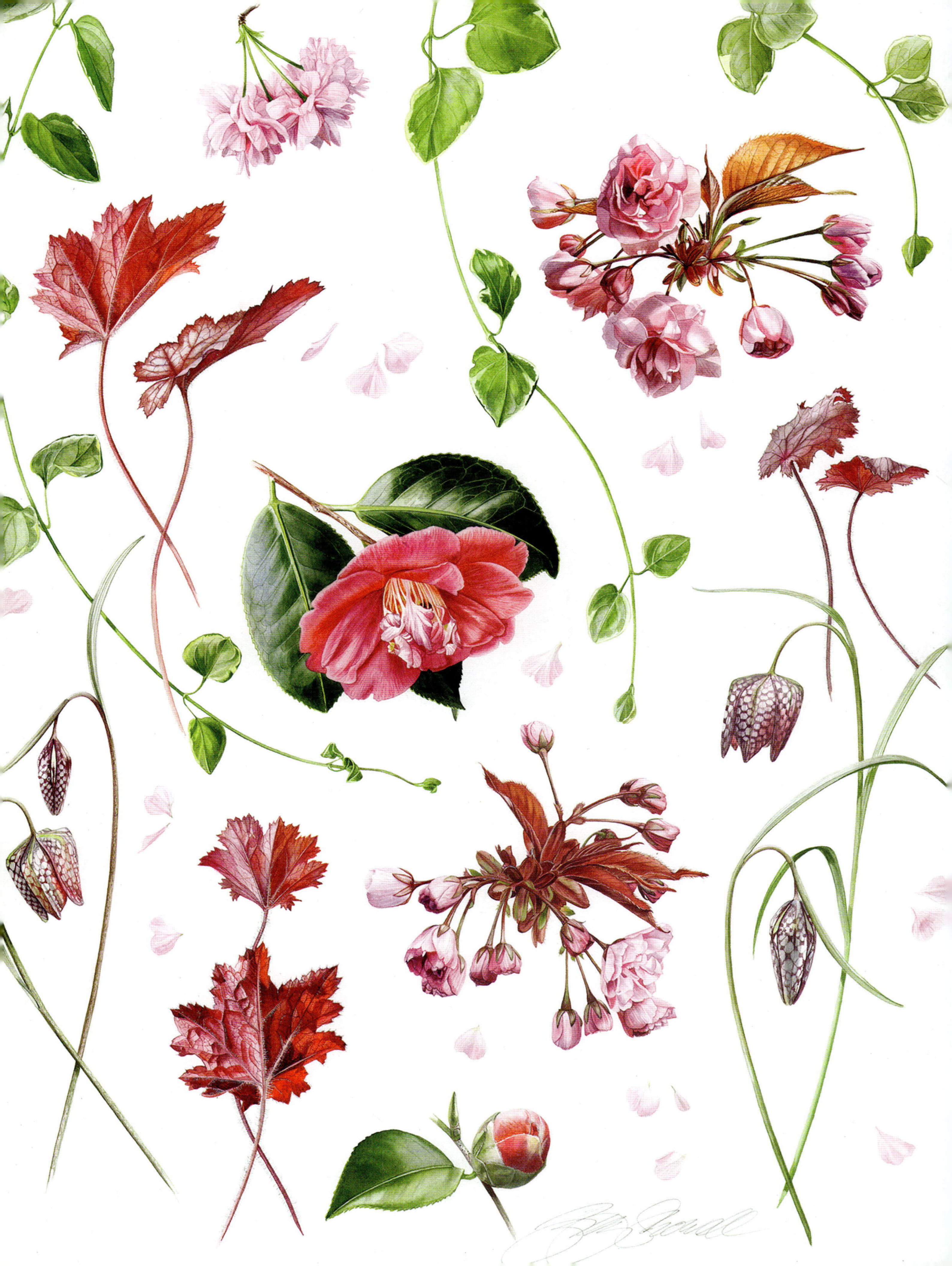

The BOTANICAL SHOES

AND THE FANTASY

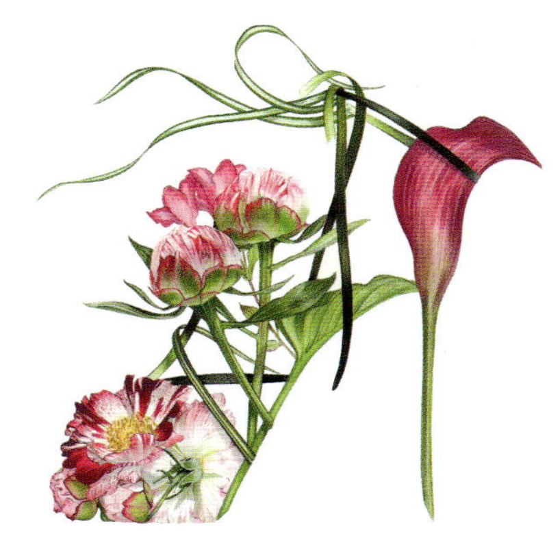

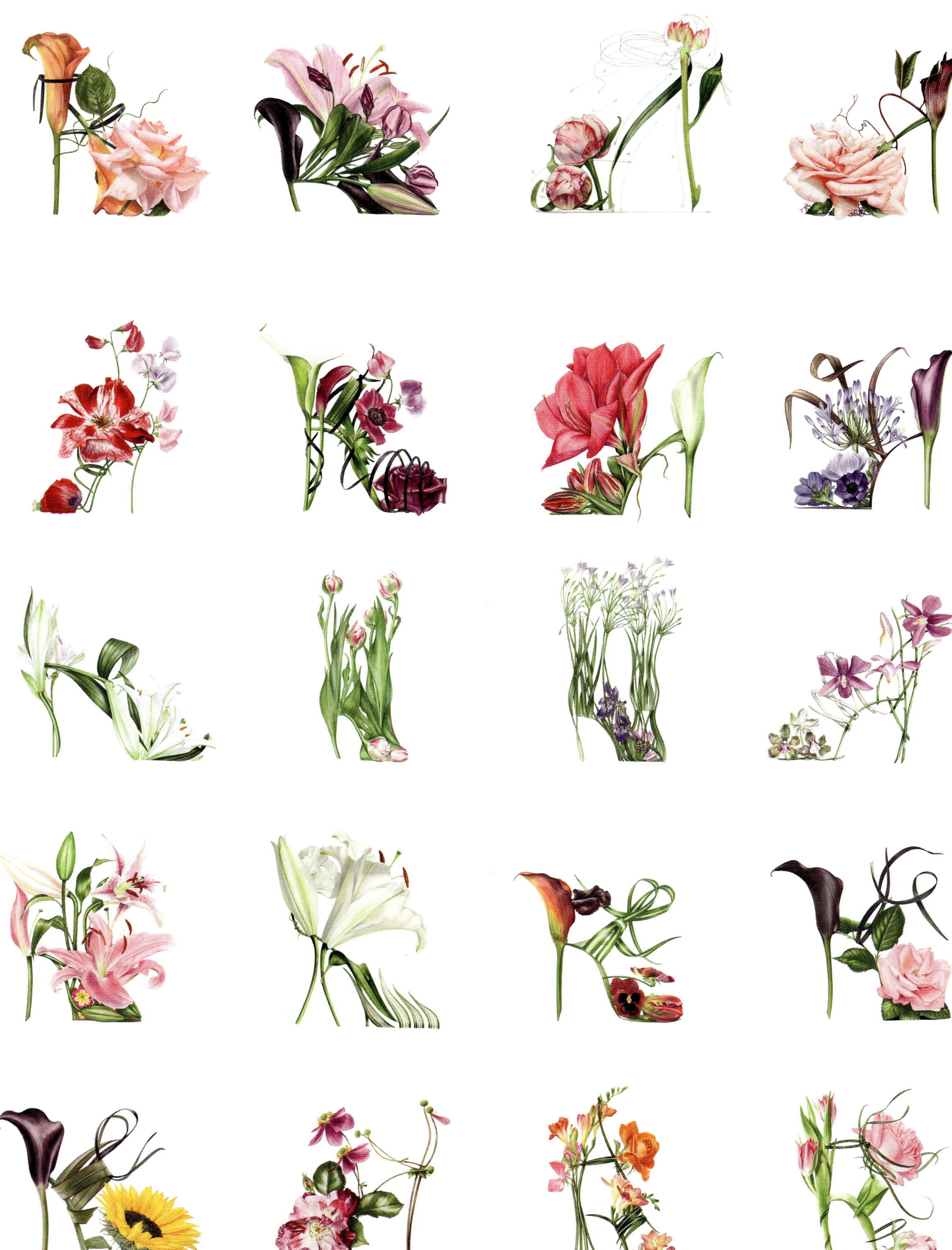

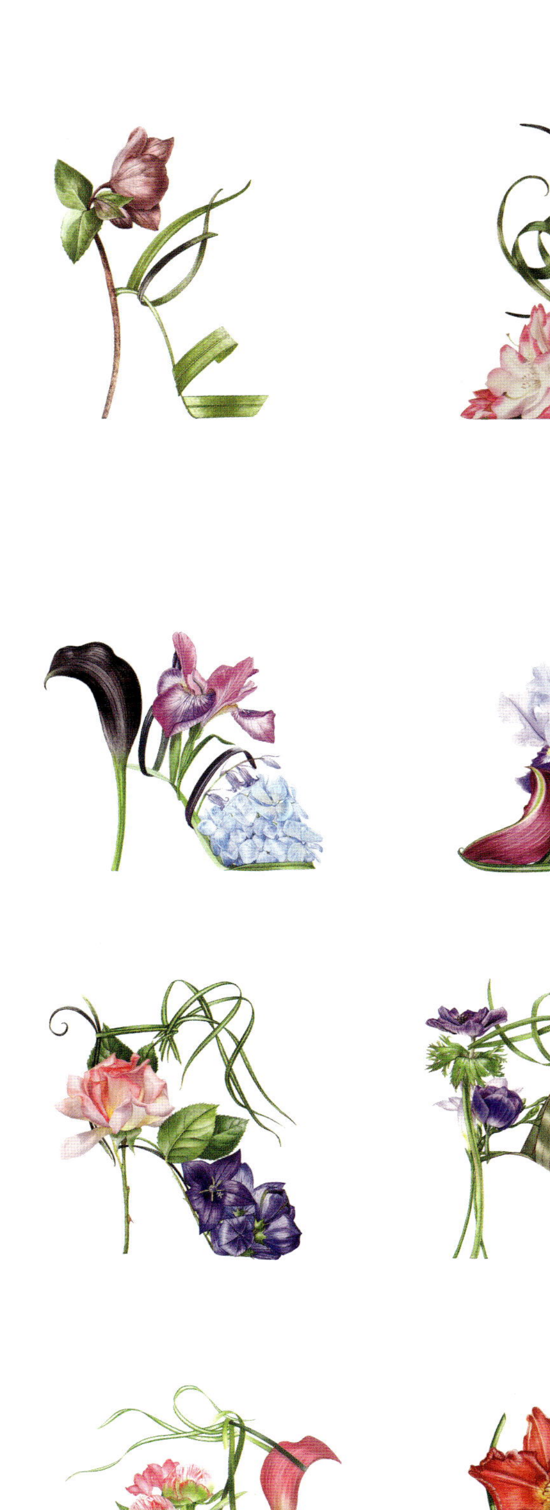
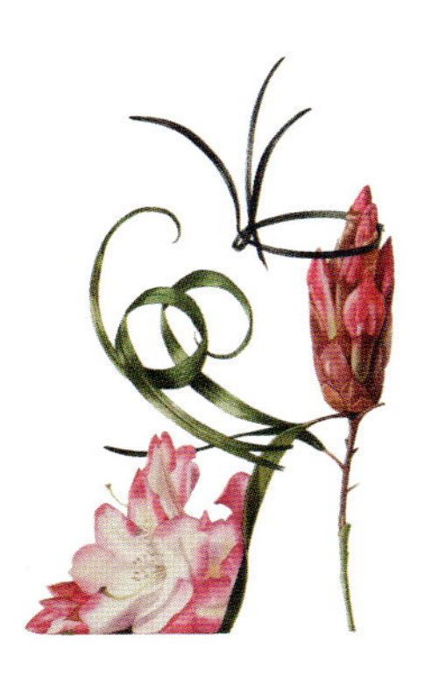
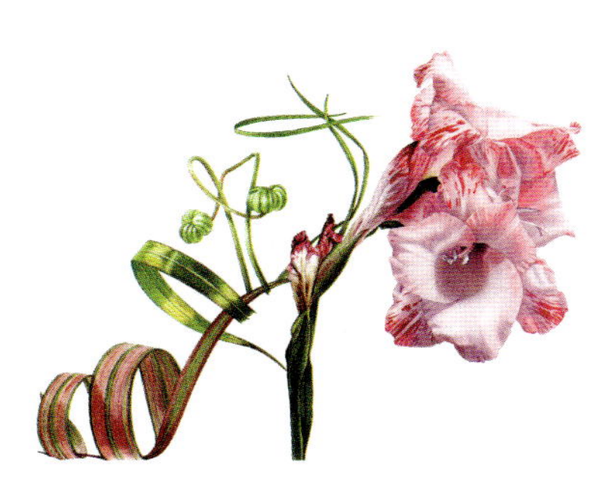
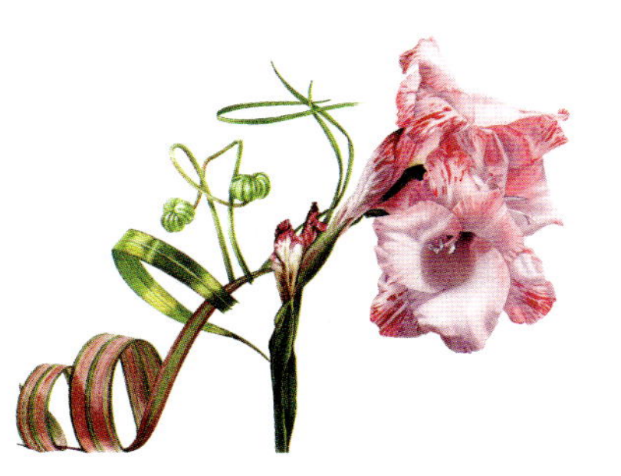
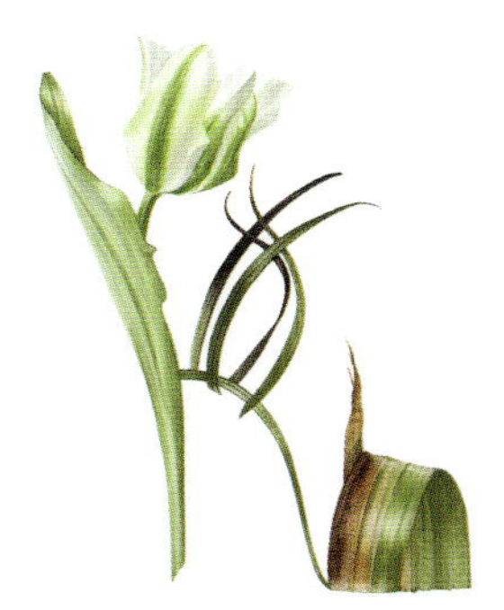
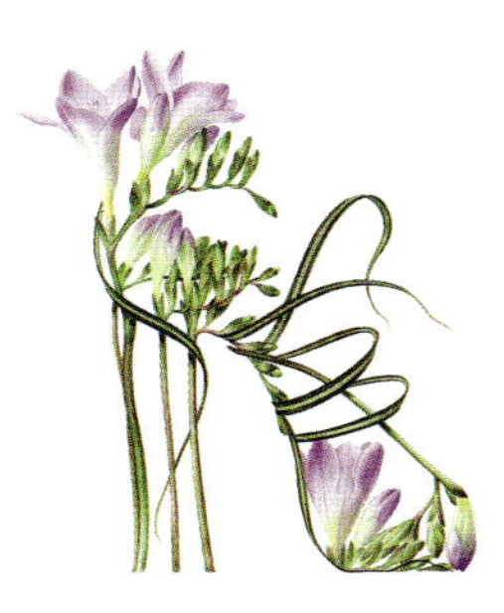
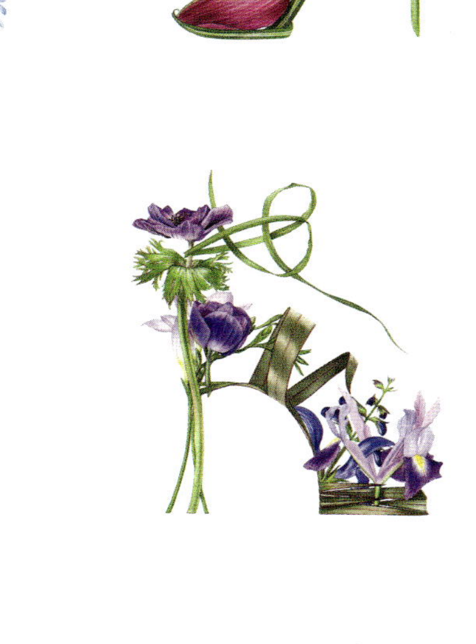
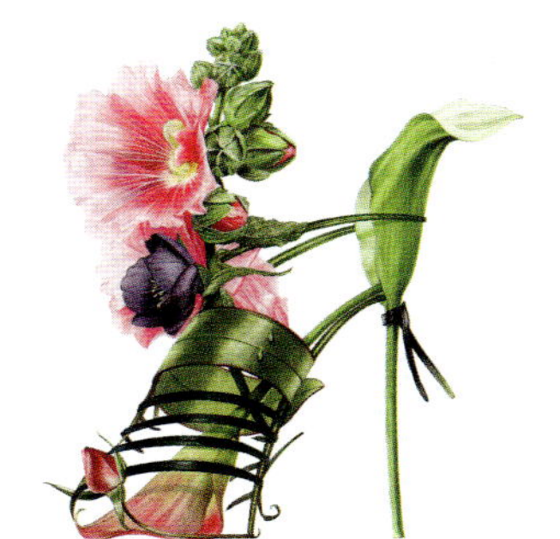
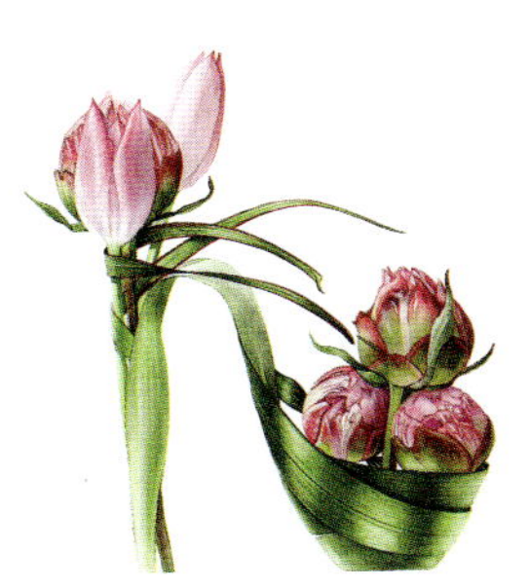
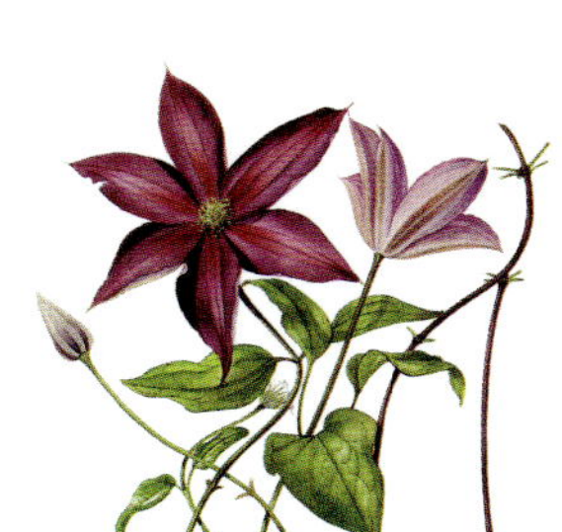
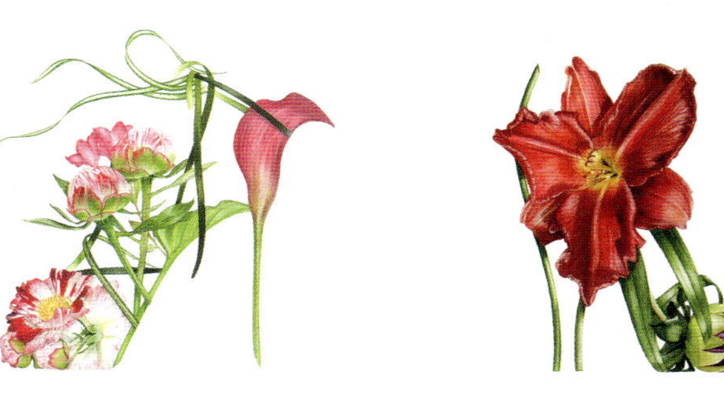
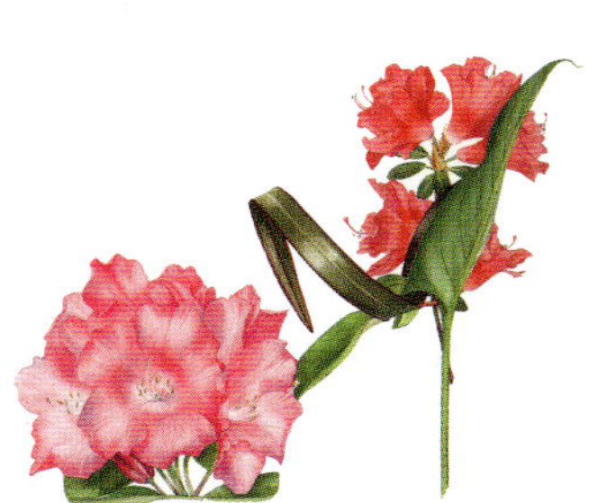
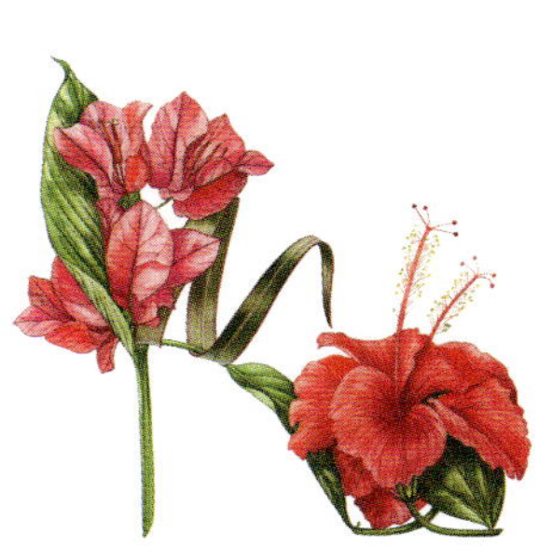
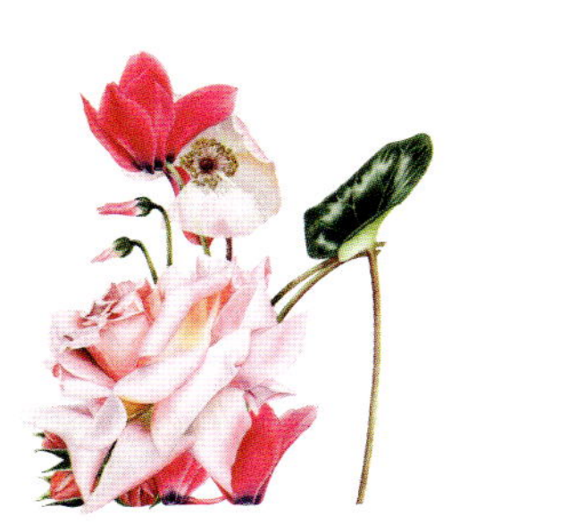
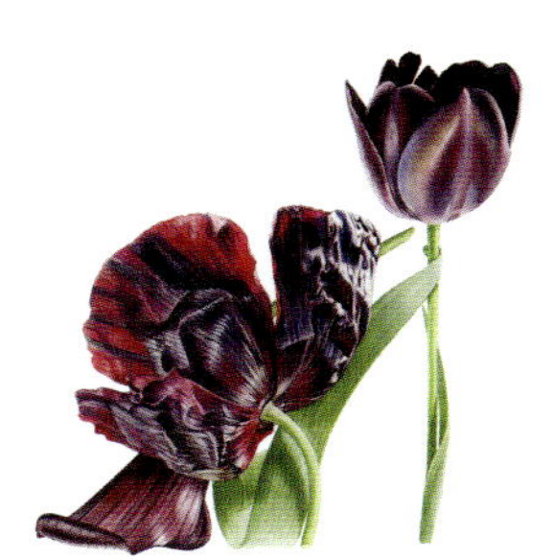
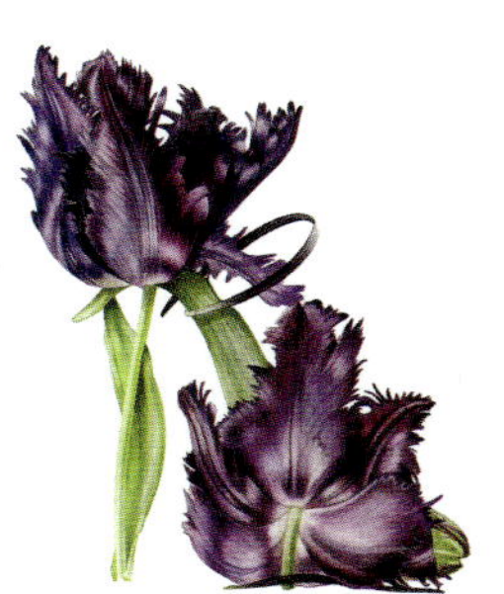

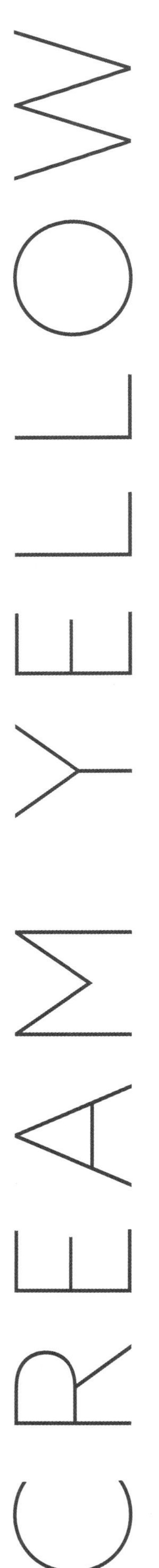

THE WAY

I start with my palette,
The colours need names
That reflect the true nature and soul.
I begin with the pale
As they will bring light
Then saffron that leads onto gold.

LOVE COLOUR

My colour palettes throughout this book are named for mood and not analysis. Colour is exciting to play with and mix. Always use good artist-quality pigments and practise for joy.

We love the crisp white of daisy petals shining out against their buttery centres, the luscious sunflower yellow and the joy of a momentary, gold, gossamer sunbeam.

More happiness can be found in the mellow light reaching from the centre of a cream rose and the sparkling glint of a sunset's reflection in a pool. The colour of morning mist can be a pale hint of perfection.

Yellow is happiest amongst its own hues, so mix only the palest of shadows to sit beneath them. Paint deeper areas in stronger, warmer shades of yellow to keep the colours true.

The first shoes are visions of what is to come
pale and green or golden like sun.

CREAM YELLOWS

S. = Sennelier

COLUMN ONE	COLUMN TWO
S. Lemon + S. Rose madder	S. Lemon
S. Lemon + S. Rose madder + S. Cobalt blue	S. Lemon + S. Yellow deep
S. Dioxazine purple + S. Quinacridone gold	S. Lemon + S. Red orange
S. Dioxazine purple + S. Quinacridone gold + S. Cobalt blue	S. Yellow deep + S. Red orange
S. Quinacridone red + S. Phthalocyanine blue + S. Yellow deep	S. Yellow deep + S. Red orange + S. Lemon
S. Rose madder + S. Yellow deep + S. French ultramarine	S. Lemon + S. Quinacridone gold
S. French ultramarine + S. Red + S. Yellow deep	S. Quinacridone gold + S. Yellow deep
S. Cobalt blue + S. Yellow deep + S. Red	S. Quinacridone gold + S. Red orange
S. Phthalocyanine blue + S. Lemon + S. Red	S. Quinacridone gold + S. Red orange + S. Lemon

COLUMN ONE	COLUMN TWO
Pretty promise	*New light*
Fairy tooth	*Moon morning*
Warm salt	*Noon swoon*
Dirty daisy	*Beech dapple*
Plum bloom	*Sleepy heat*
Fading rose	*Golden ash*
Buttery cloud	*Golden wand*
Sweeping rain	*Happy honey*
Apple bloom	*Treasured summer*

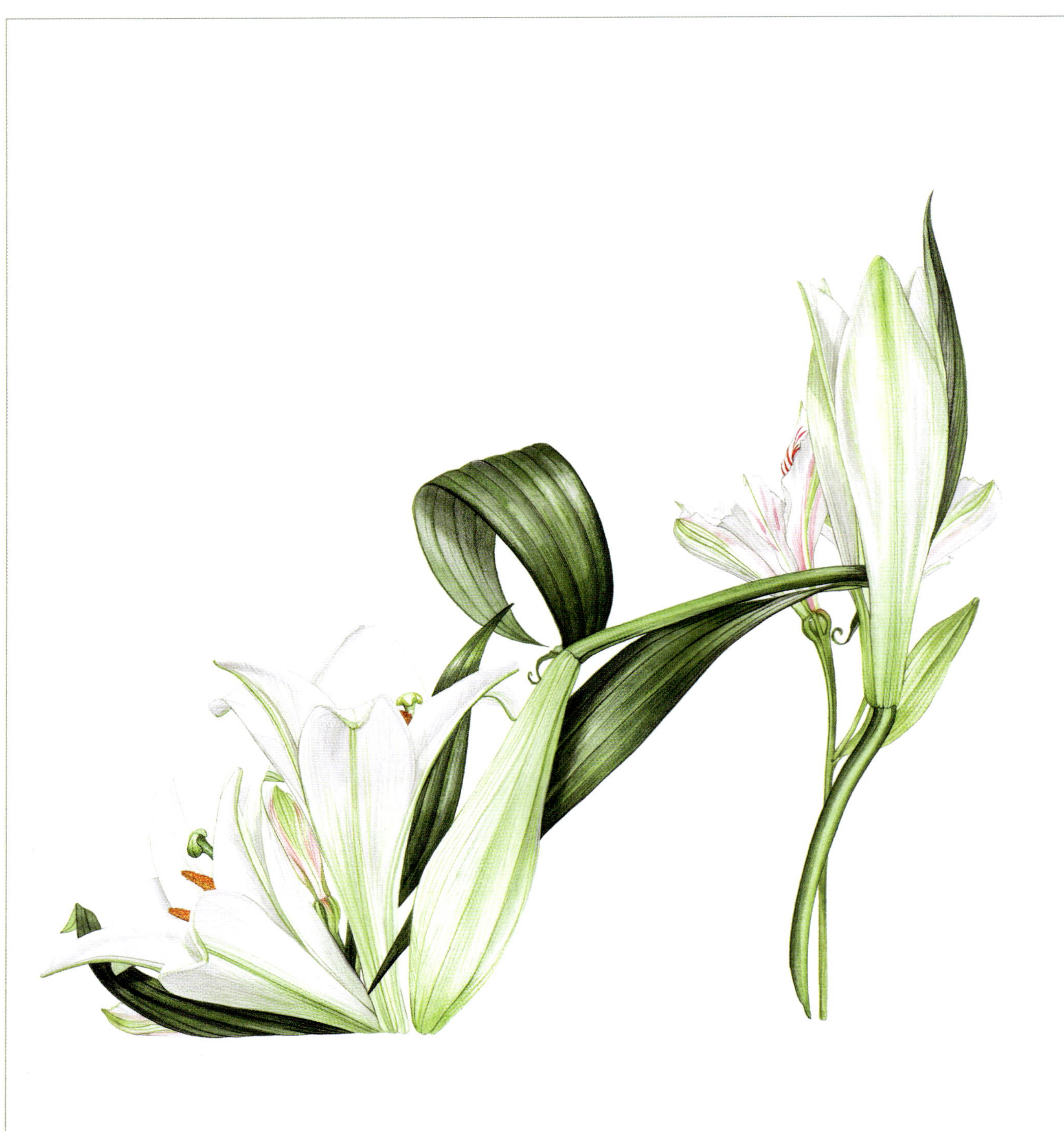

I make no excuses for my flights of fancy,
I only ask that you
dance
with me to the last page
and beyond.

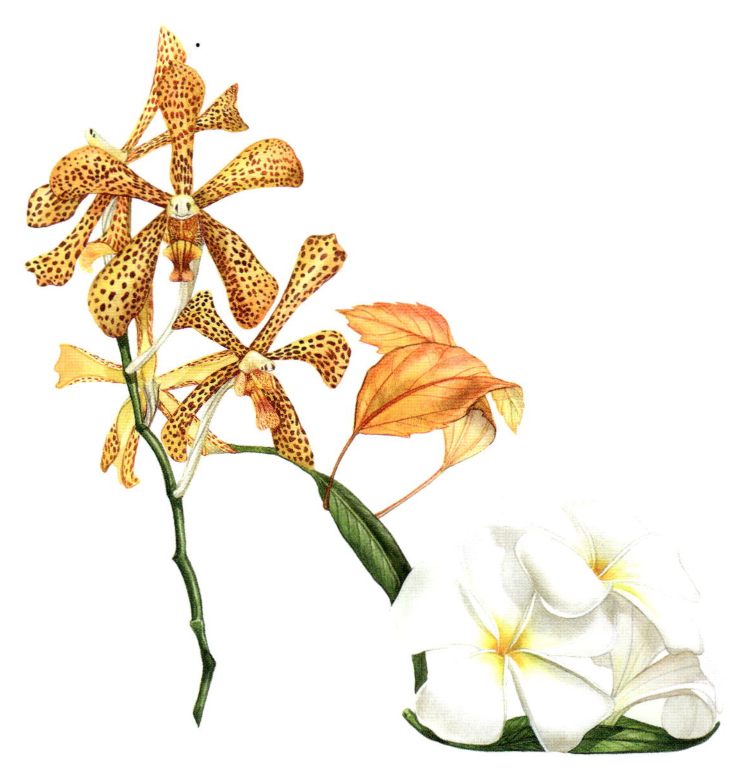

for
every
path
has
the
promise
of
prettiness

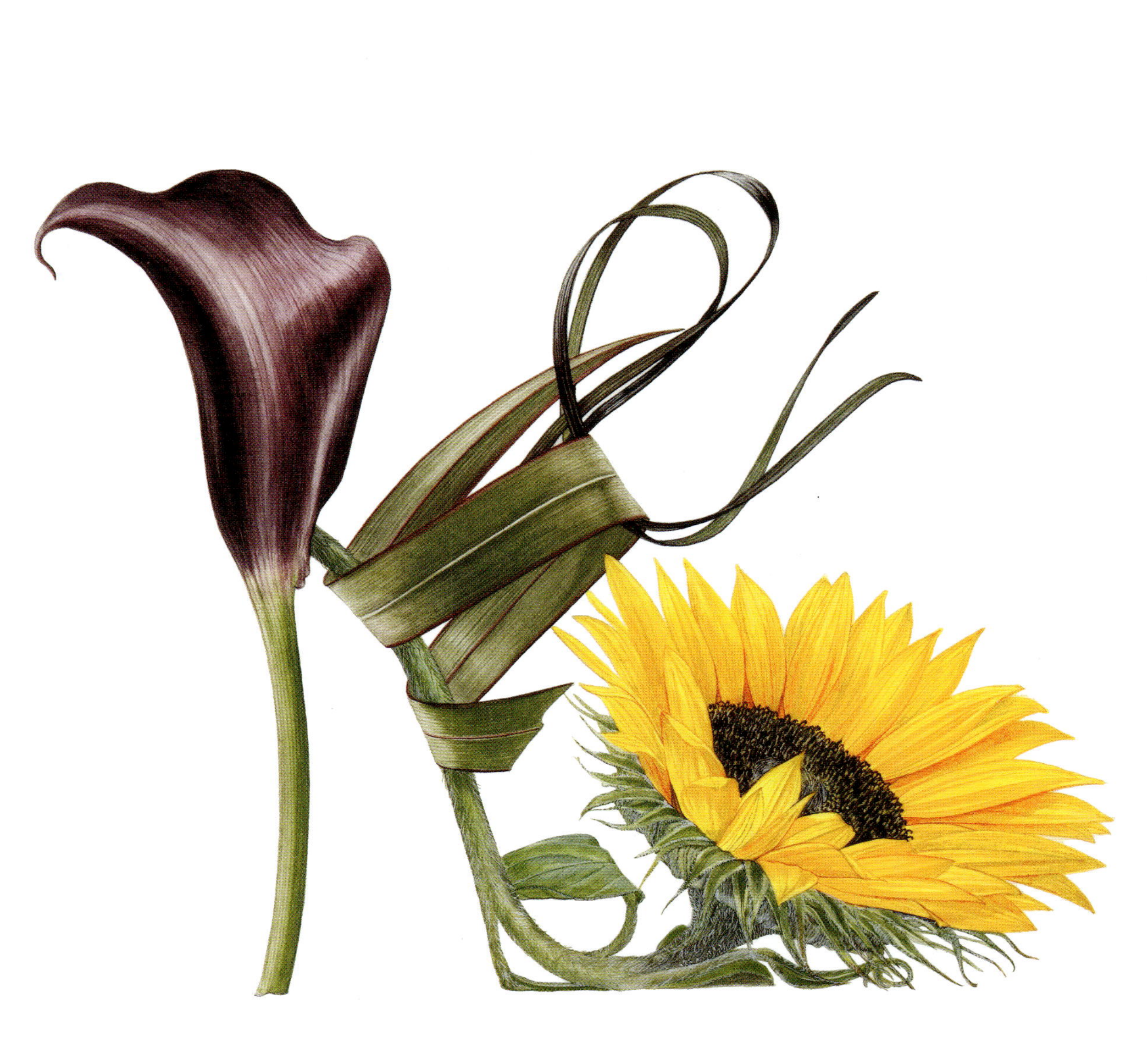

Let us run until our feet grow wings.

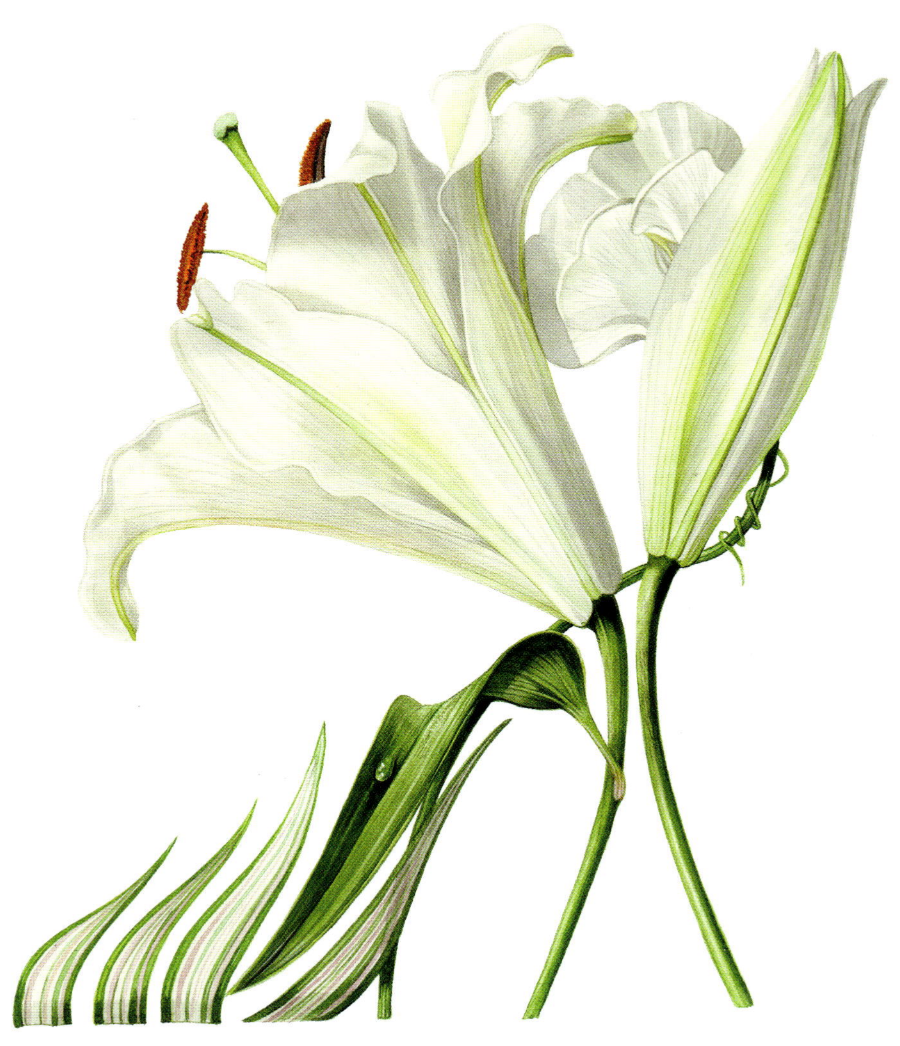

We will rest only when the light fades to tell us so.

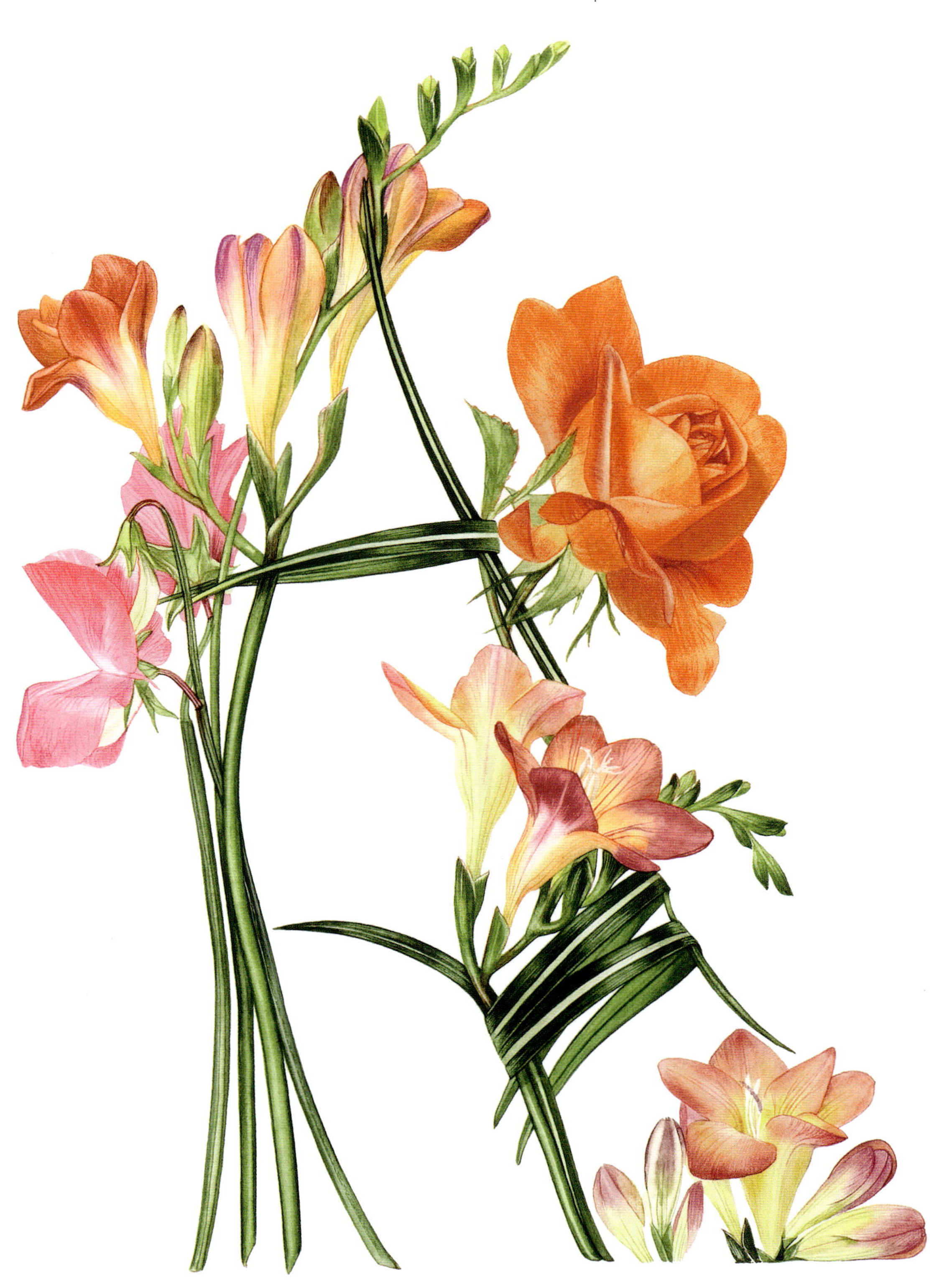

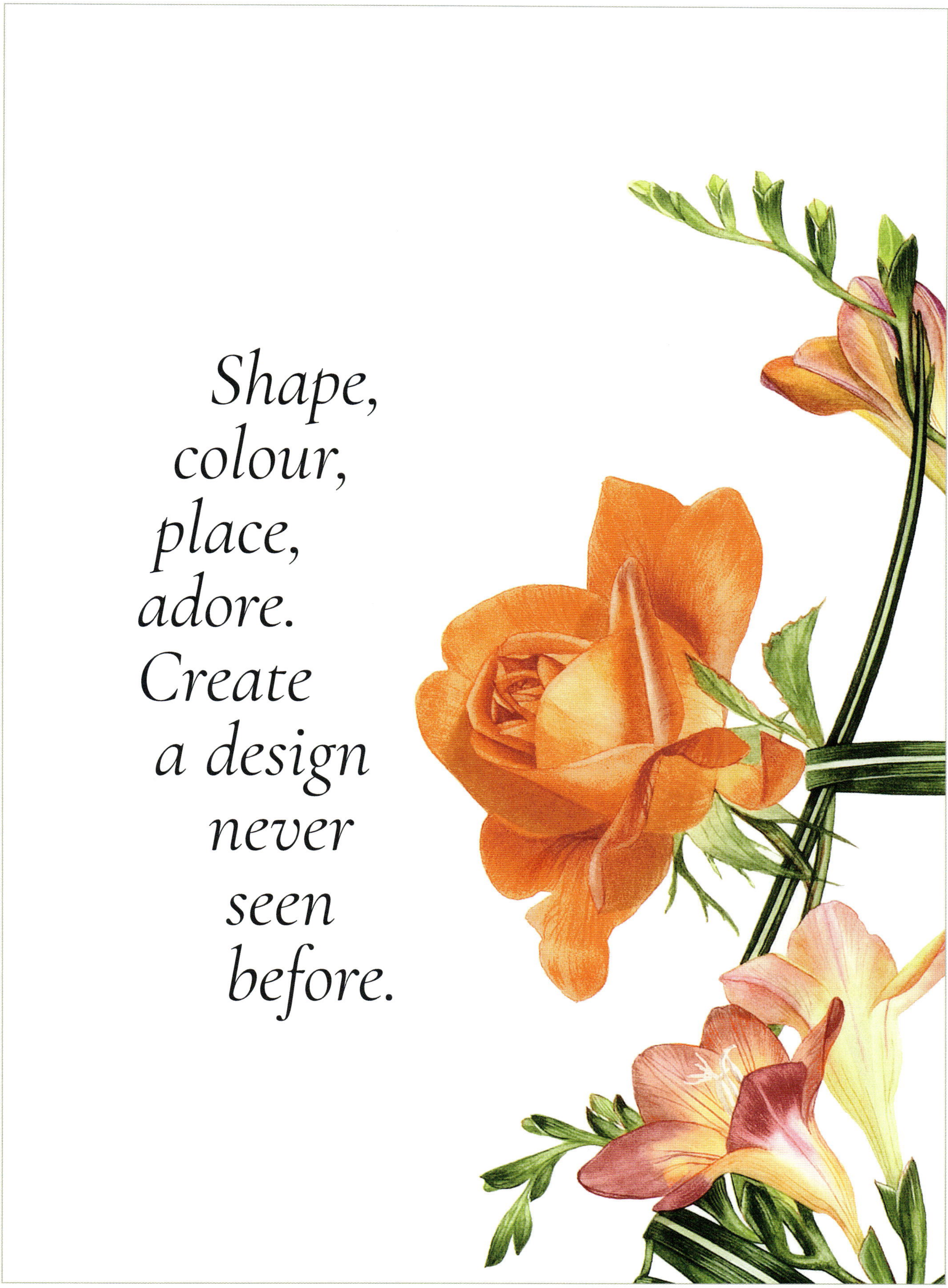

Shape,
colour,
place,
adore.
Create
a design
never
seen
before.

THE NIGHT BEFORE

Seen in a moment, tear in my eye,
I see a future to which I aspire.

Clouds of tissue paper covered the bed,
and there they sat unwrapped
the most beautiful, floral, silken slippers
made from nature perhaps imbued with magic.

TIP

Keep your mixes clean and your brush on its tippy tip-toe,
hold it low on the ferrule to assert control. You are the
master of the marks you make.

Take your brush for a dance with me.

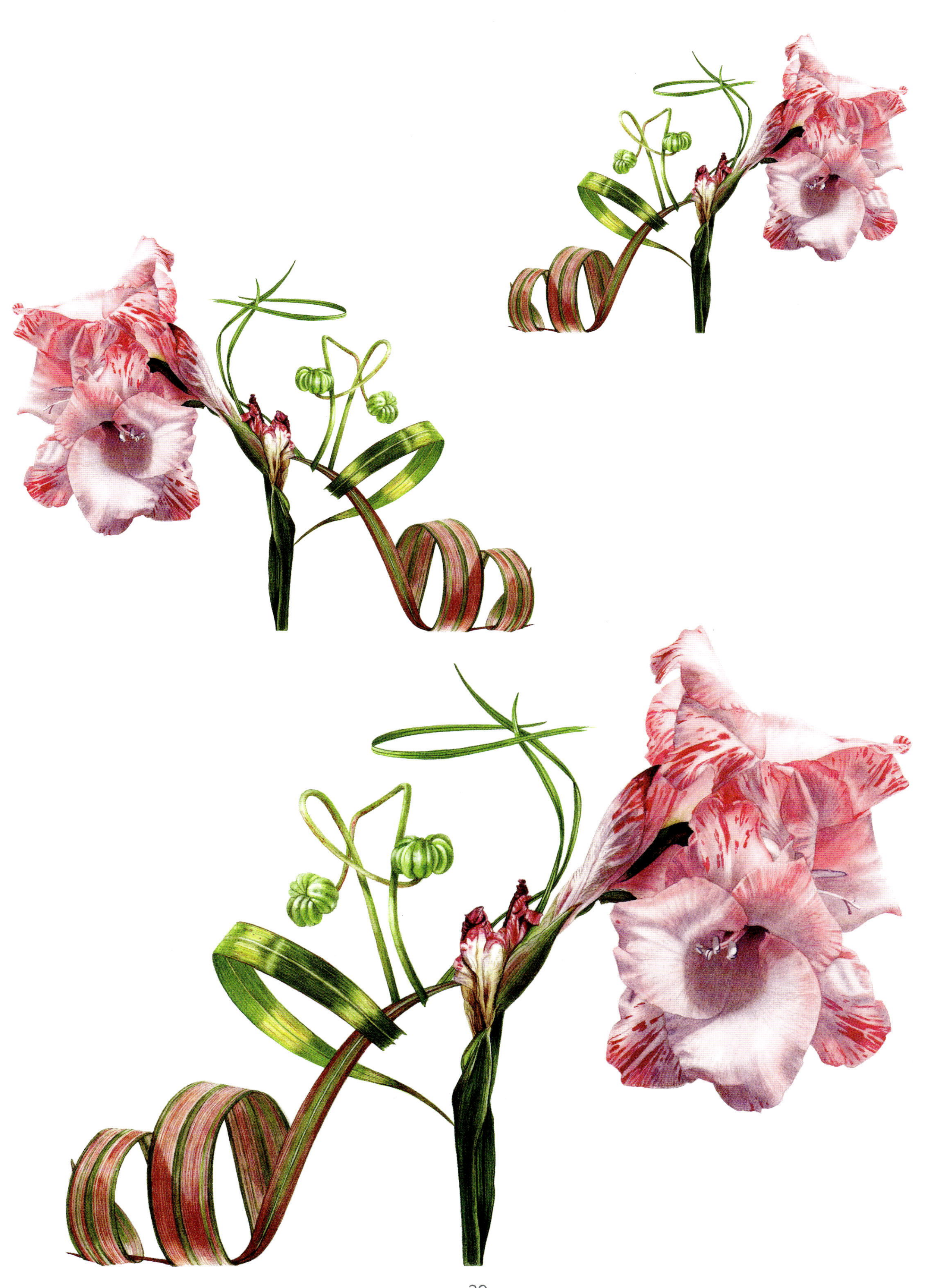

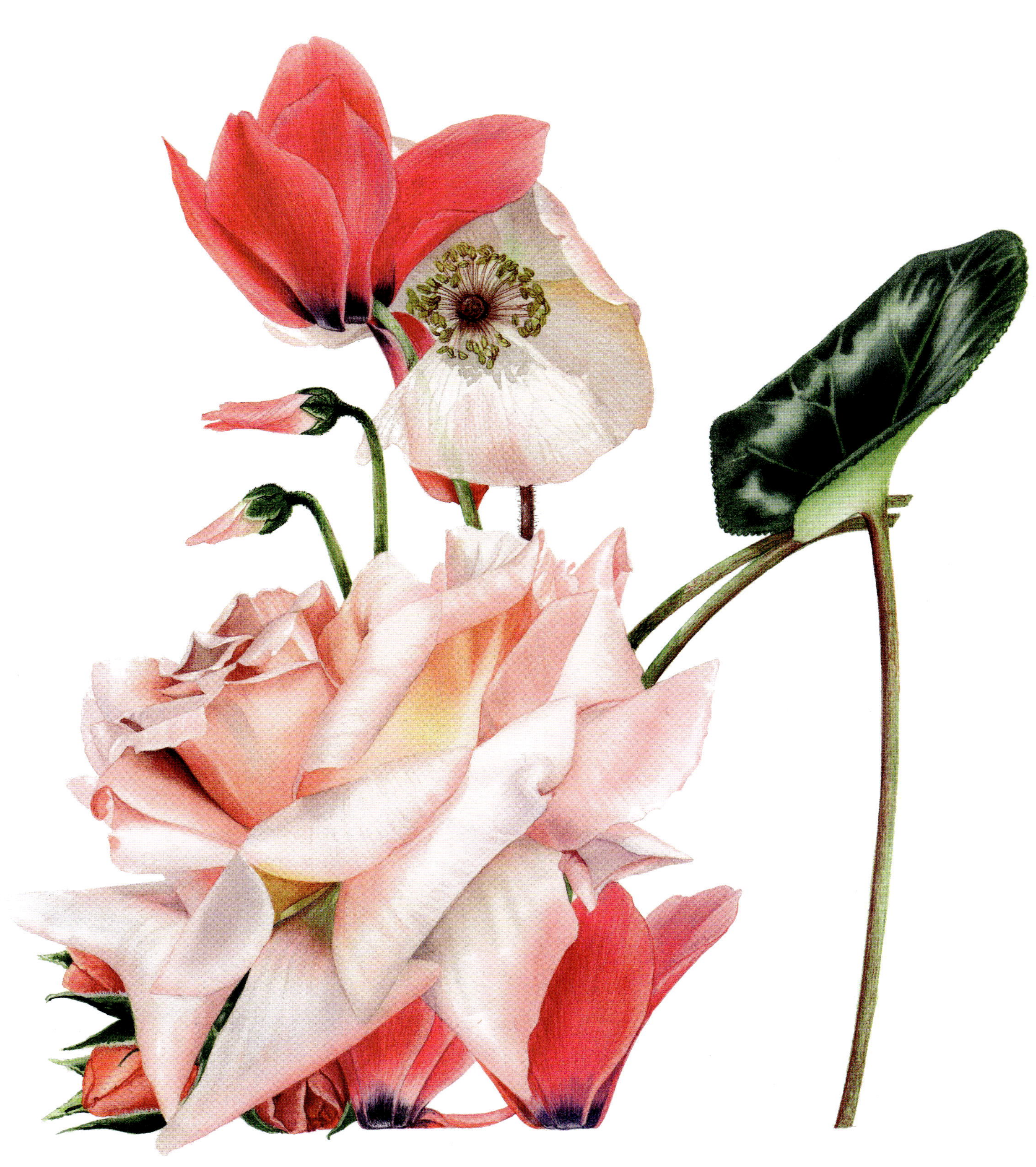

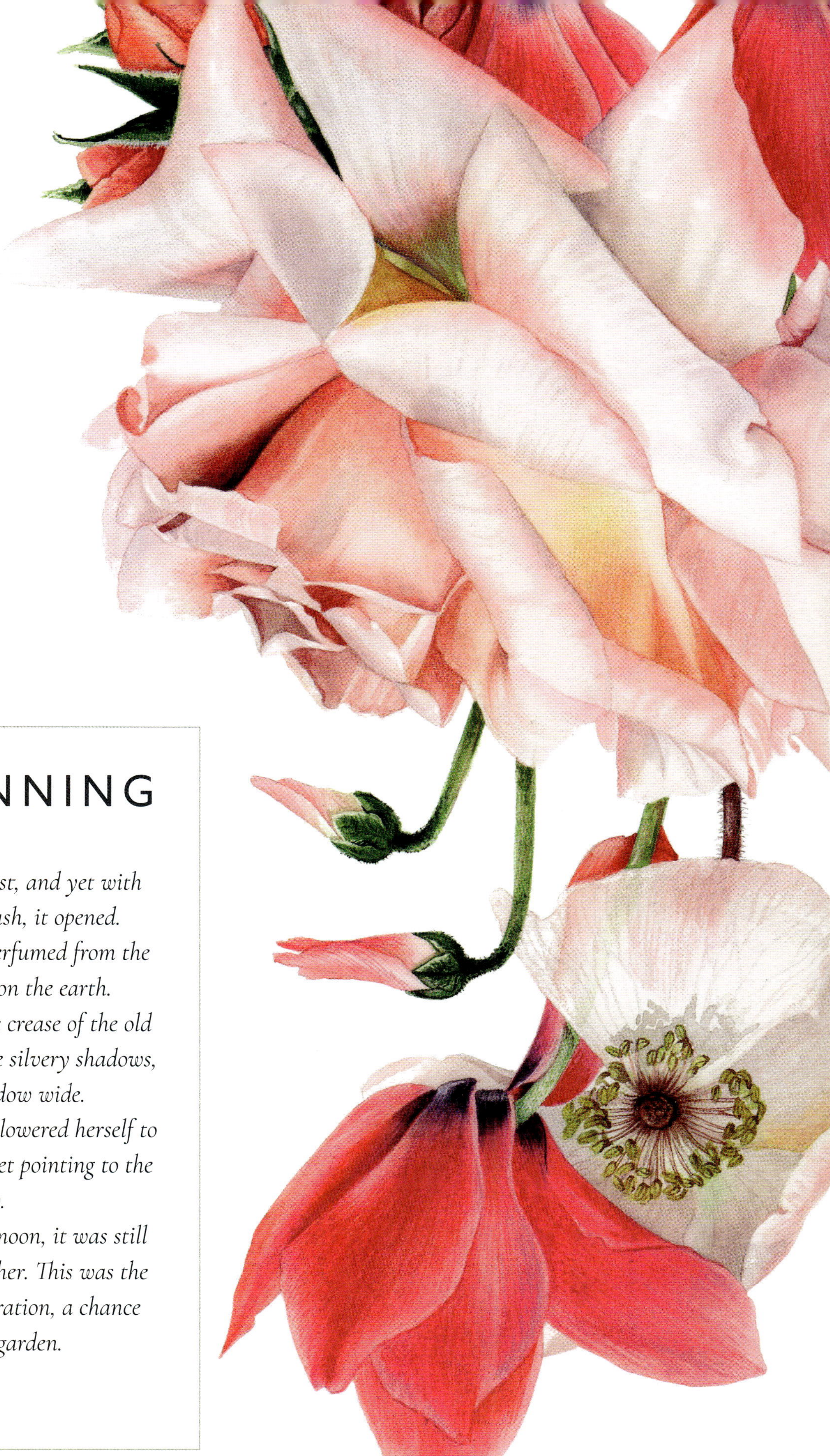

THE BEGINNING

*The window seemed stuck fast, and yet with
a quiet and determined push, it opened.
The air was sweet and still perfumed from the
touch of summer rain upon the earth.
Previously content within the crease of the old
sill, the insects scattered to the silvery shadows,
as she pushed the window wide.
Carefully she stepped up then lowered herself to
sit on the sill with her bare feet pointing to the
ground below.
Despite the light of the half-moon, it was still
very dark; no one would see her. This was the
moment, a window to exploration, a chance
perhaps to find the garden.*

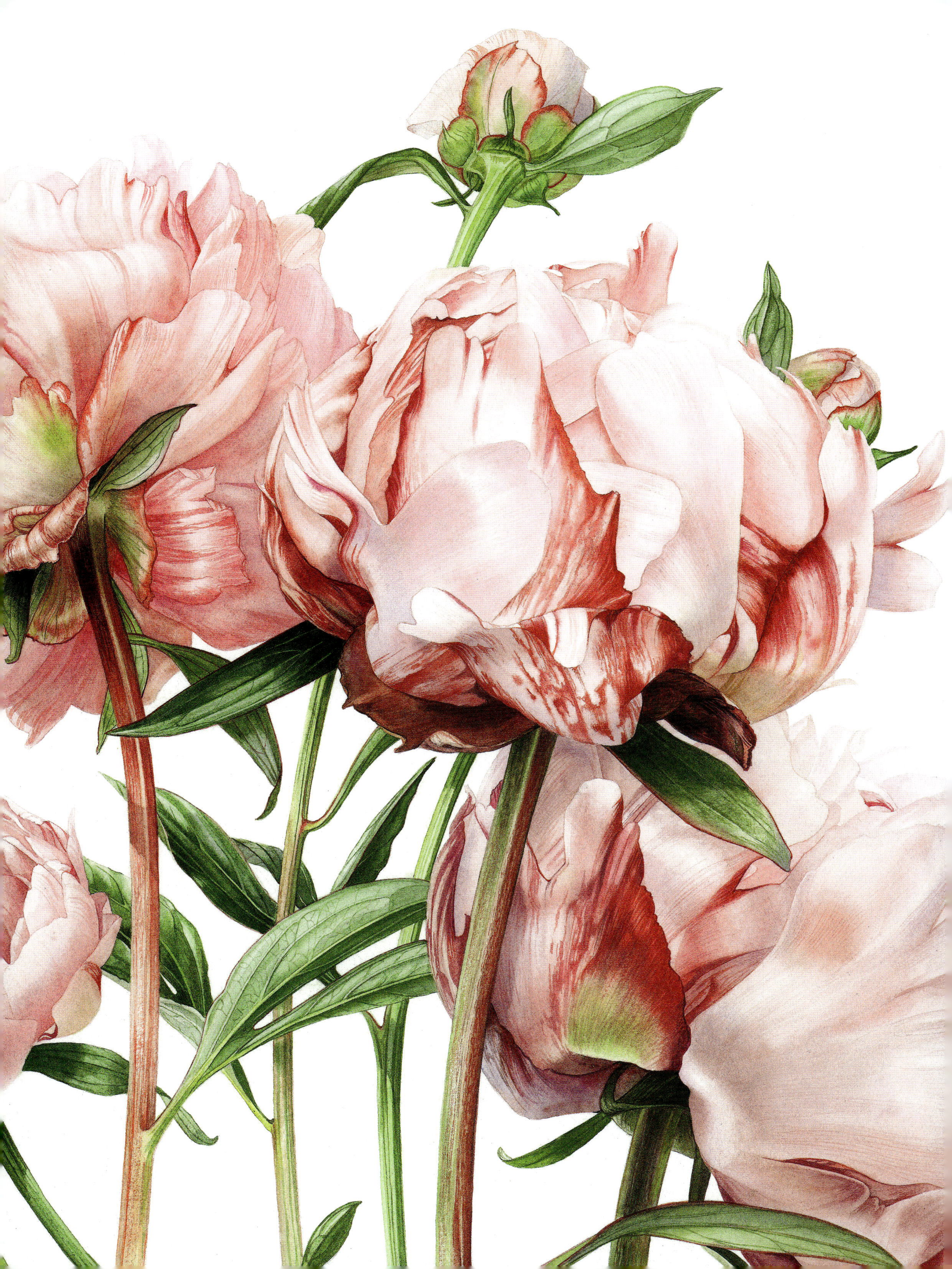

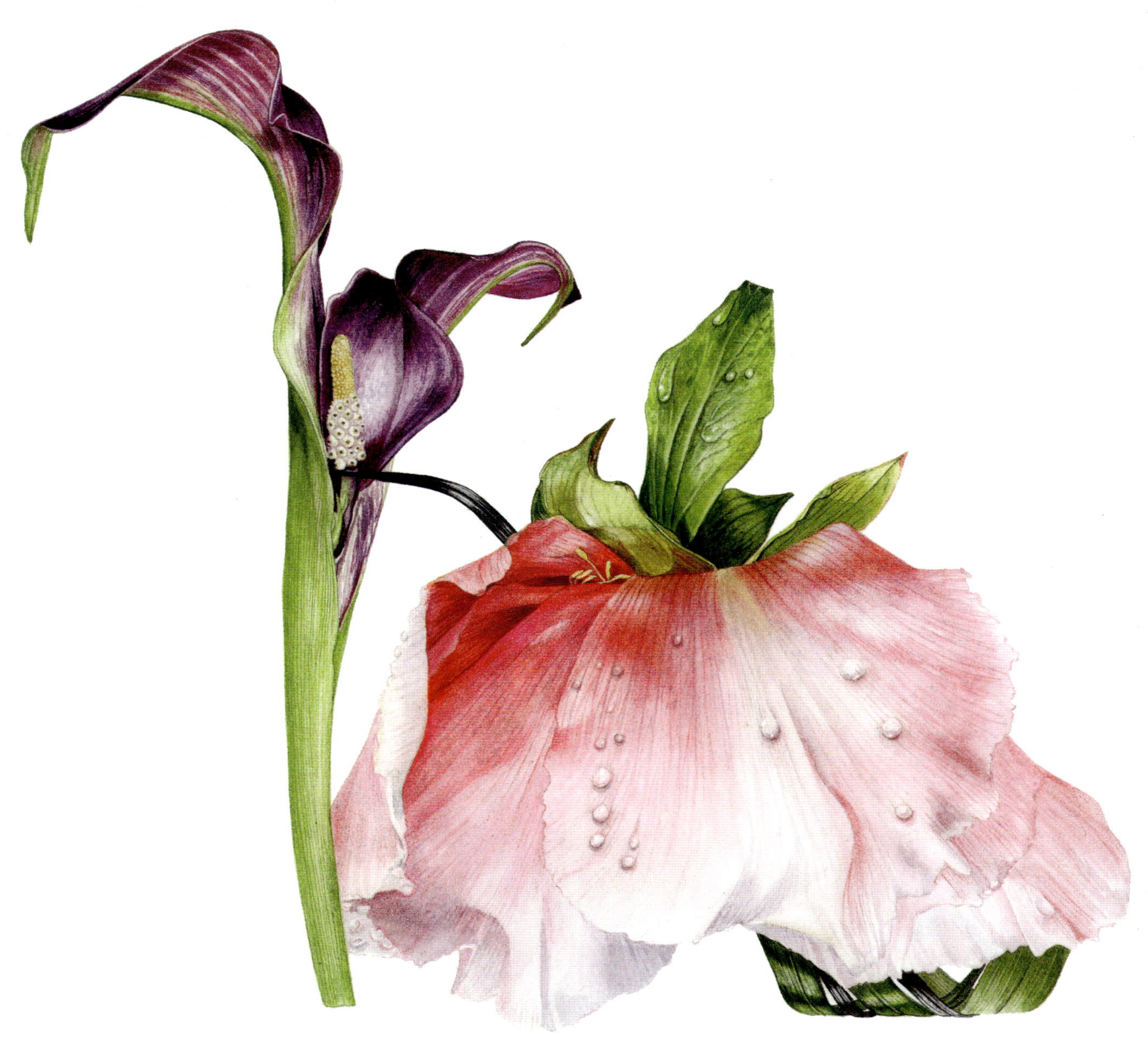

Before the birds stir, and the mist hangs in wait to settle,
your bare feet will leave dark tracks in the green,
icy, fresh, awakening.

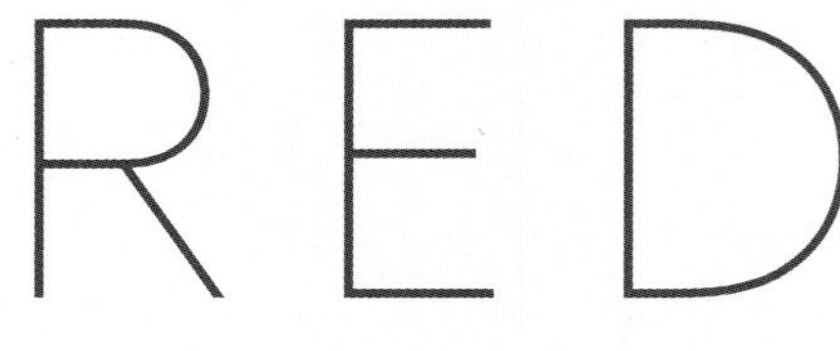

RED

Parry and be ready for all that is ahead
to assert determination, embrace the colour red.
I will go there; I will see the colours for myself.
The corner of a field where the poppies sway,
a gentle breeze and they are gone.
But I will hold that moment dear.

Some reds are pink and some maroon. Some reds are more orange and some have a hint of lilac. All reds are a delight to mix. A deep red-pink can carry your imagination, convey a passion and illuminate your mood. For dark reds, mix red with pink and a touch of purple. To make red warmer, add yellow.

Keep bright reds clear and mix with quinacridone red. Make pale cool pinks by watering down Helios purple, and for warmer pinks add lemon. For heat, add some red-orange and for a hotter, orange-red, add lemon.

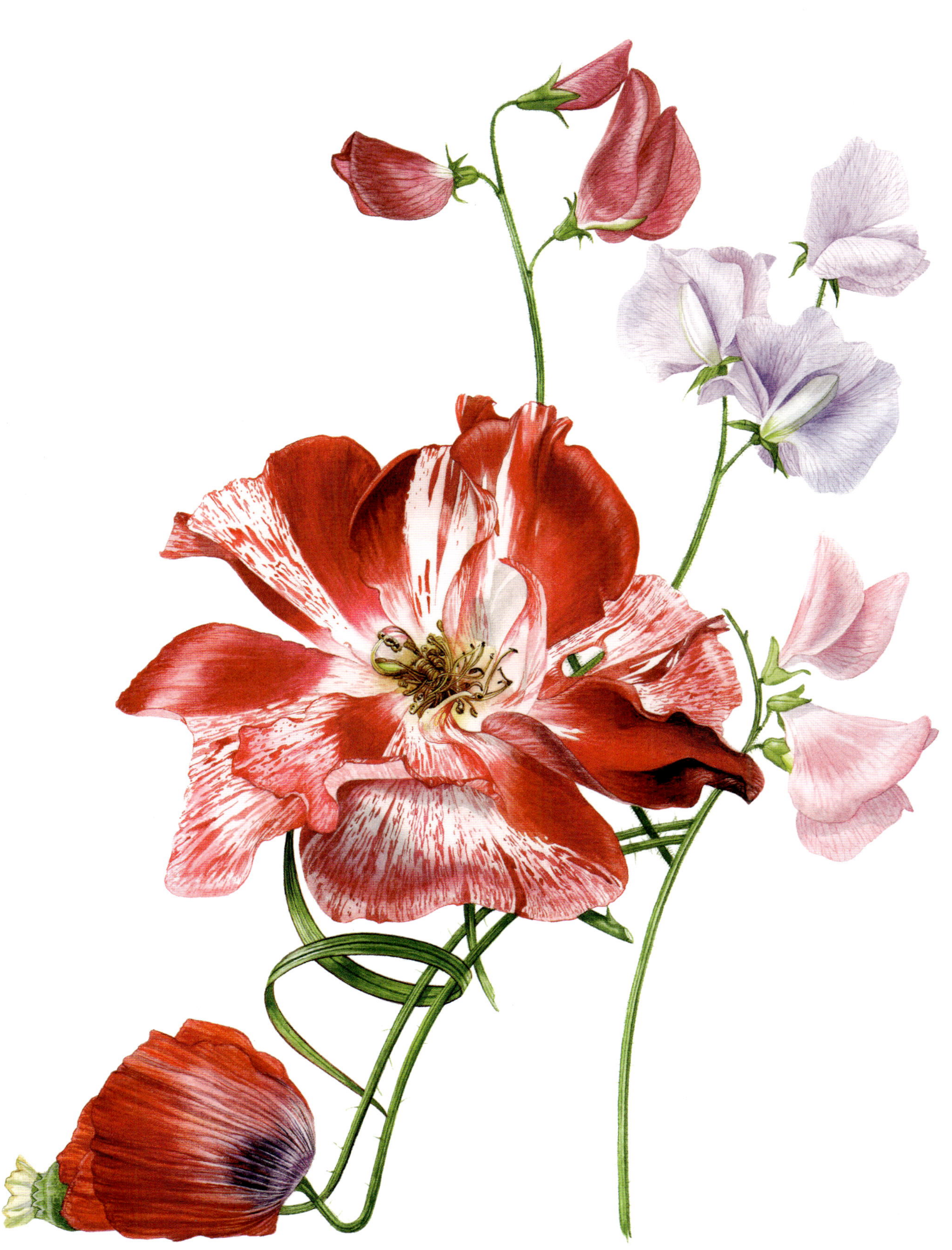

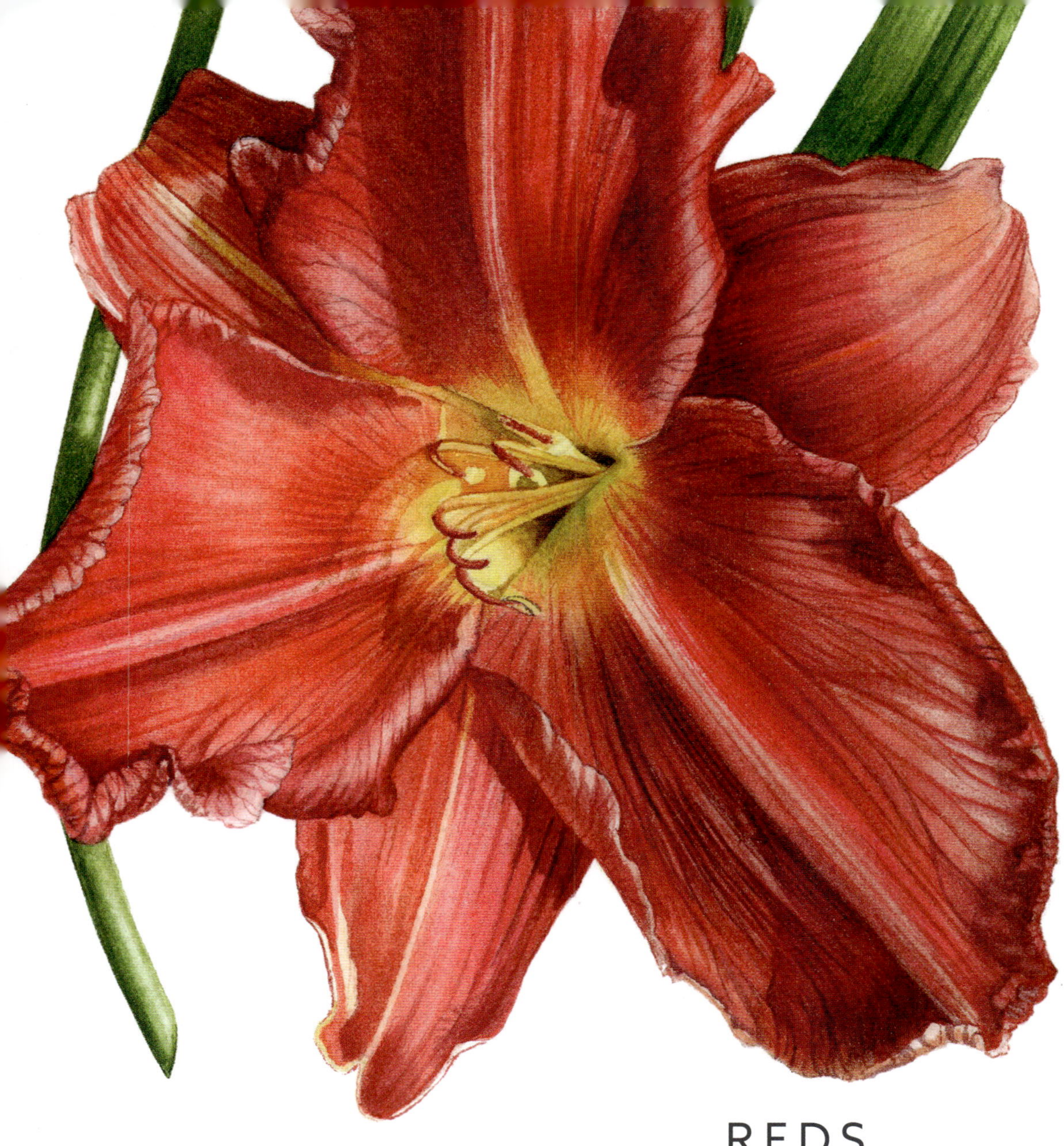

REDS

S. = Sennelier

COLUMN ONE

S. Red + S. Helios purple

S. Red + S. Dioxazine purple

S. Red + S. Dioxazine purple + S. Rose madder

S. Rose madder + S. Red

S. Red + S. Rose madder + S. Helios purple

S. Rose madder + S. Red orange + S. Dioxazine purple

S. Quinacridone red + S. Dioxazine

S. Quinacridone red + S. Dioxazine purple + S. Red

S. Red + S. Cobalt blue + S. Quinacridone red

COLUMN TWO

S. Quinacridone red

S. Quinacridone red + S. Lemon

S. Quinacridone red + S. Yellow deep

S. Quinacridone red + S. Yellow deep + S. Rose madder

S. Red + S. Yellow deep

S. Quinacridone red + S. Quinacridone gold + S. Red

S. Red + S. Quinacridone gold + S. French ultramarine

S. Rose madder + S. Yellow deep + S. French ultramarine

S. Rose madder + S. Red orange + S. French ultramarine

Raspberry cream

Plum cream

Baked blush

Berry baby

Berry juice

Hibernation

Pink pocket

Piquant cream velvet

Temptation

Coral bliss

Peach slipper

Coral carrot

Blood orange cream

Red cocoon

Sunrise

Red sea

Rare wine

Red nectar

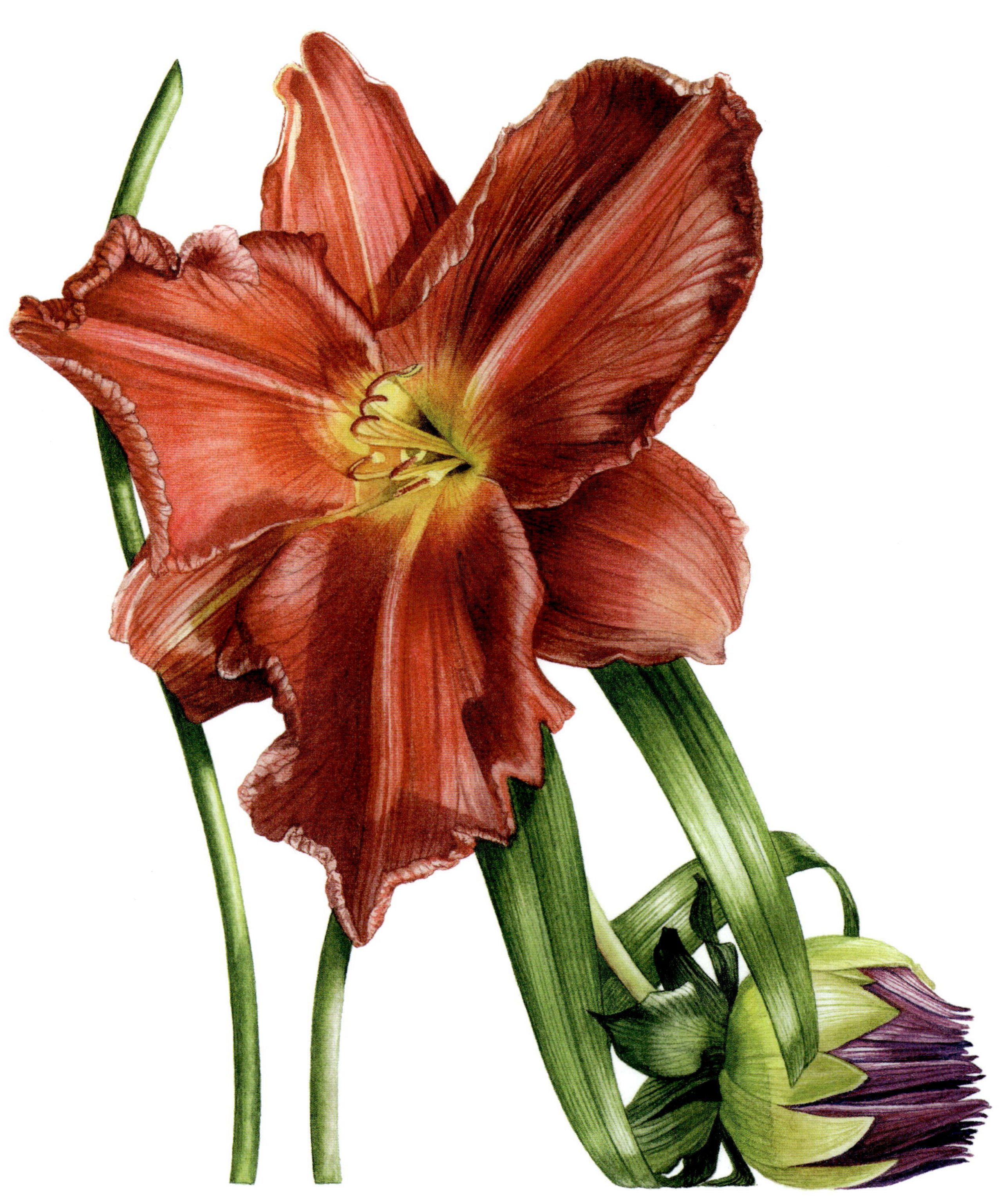

My skirt skimmed the forest floor, and as I walked, the toes of my floral
shoes peeped rhythmically from beneath the hem, no sound at all, apart
from the delicious swish of the cloth as it swept away the leaves.

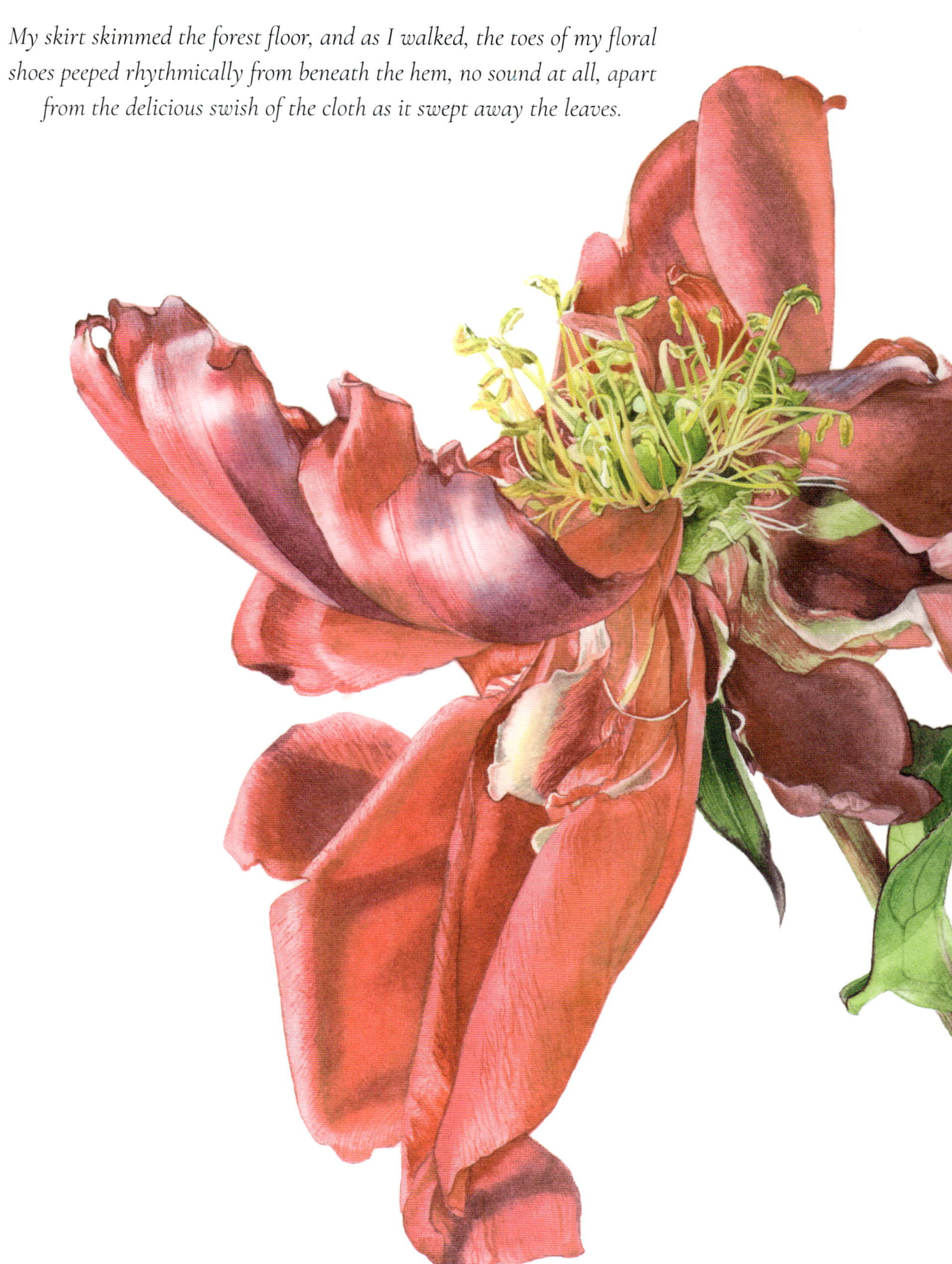

Kindness begins in the mirror,
Then on to all you meet along your way,
And in all you do, reflected in all you say.
Take it with you, push it forward every single day.

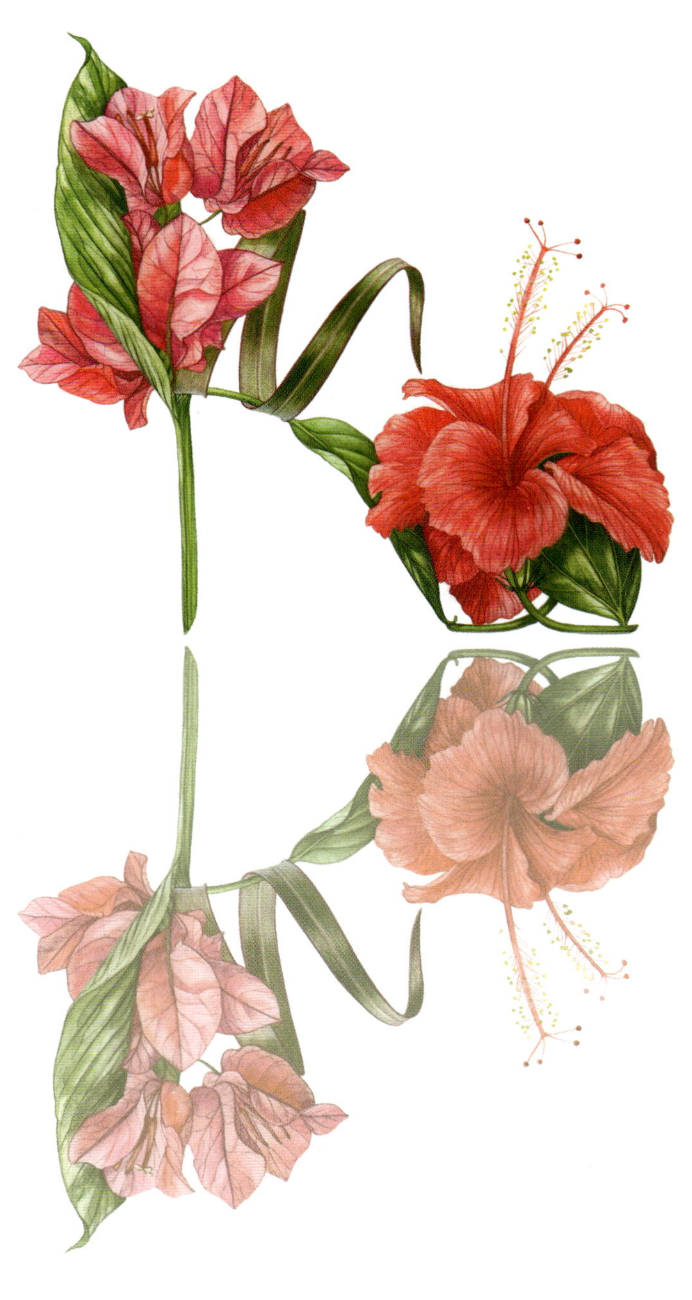

There is no shame in changing direction,
as long as you choose the path to happiness.
Remember each bloom, be thankful that they shone for you.

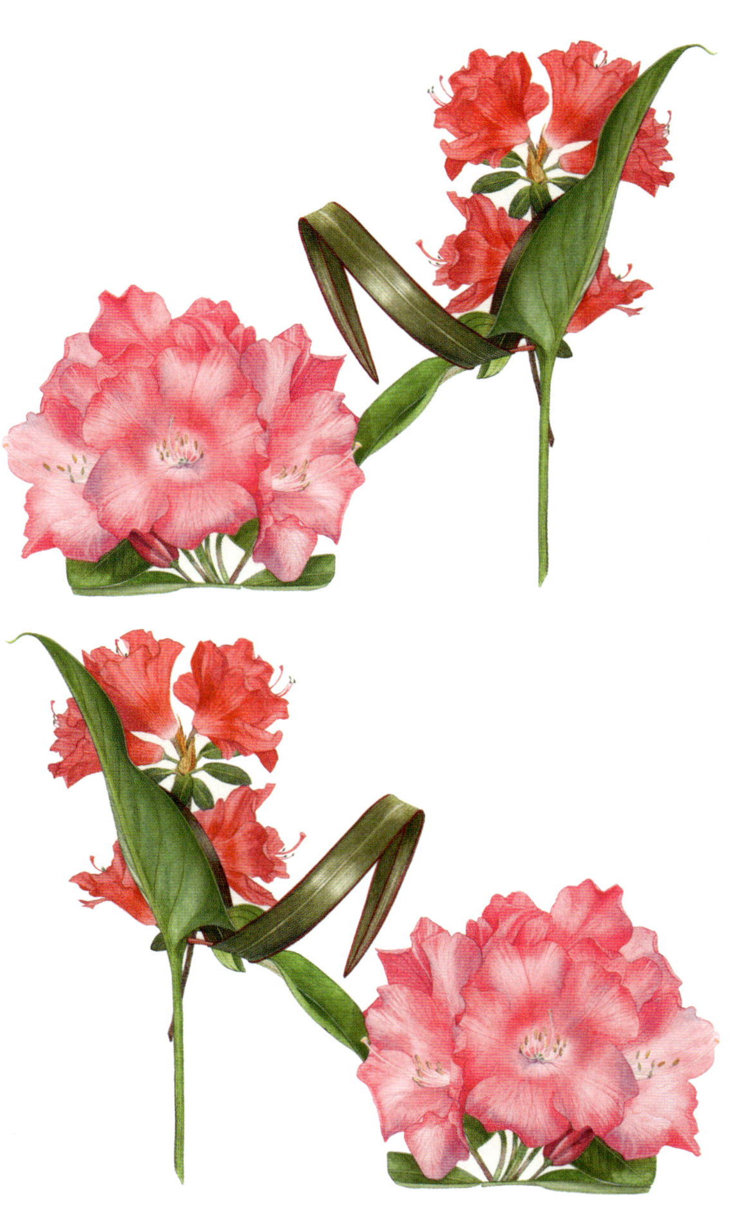

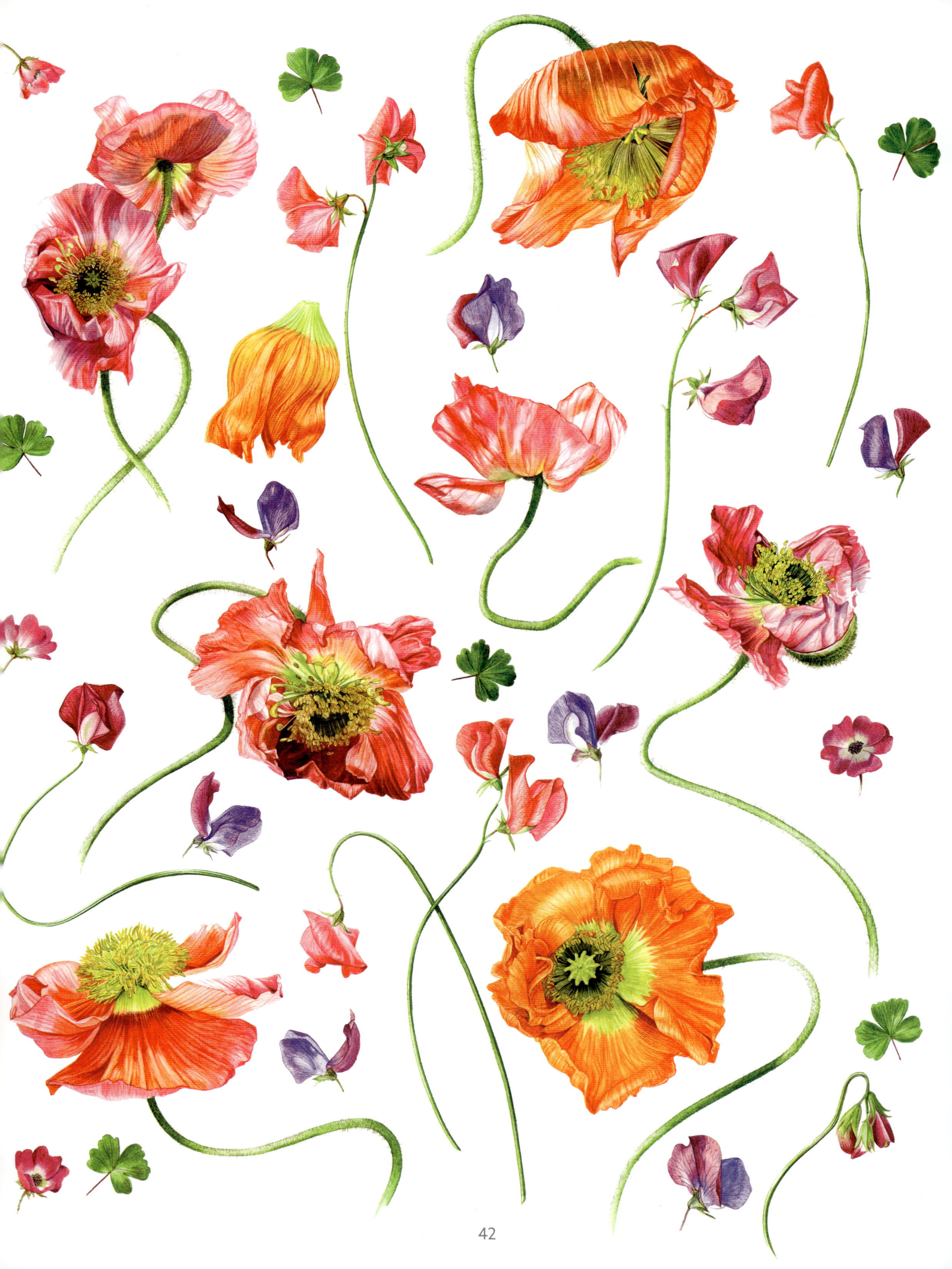

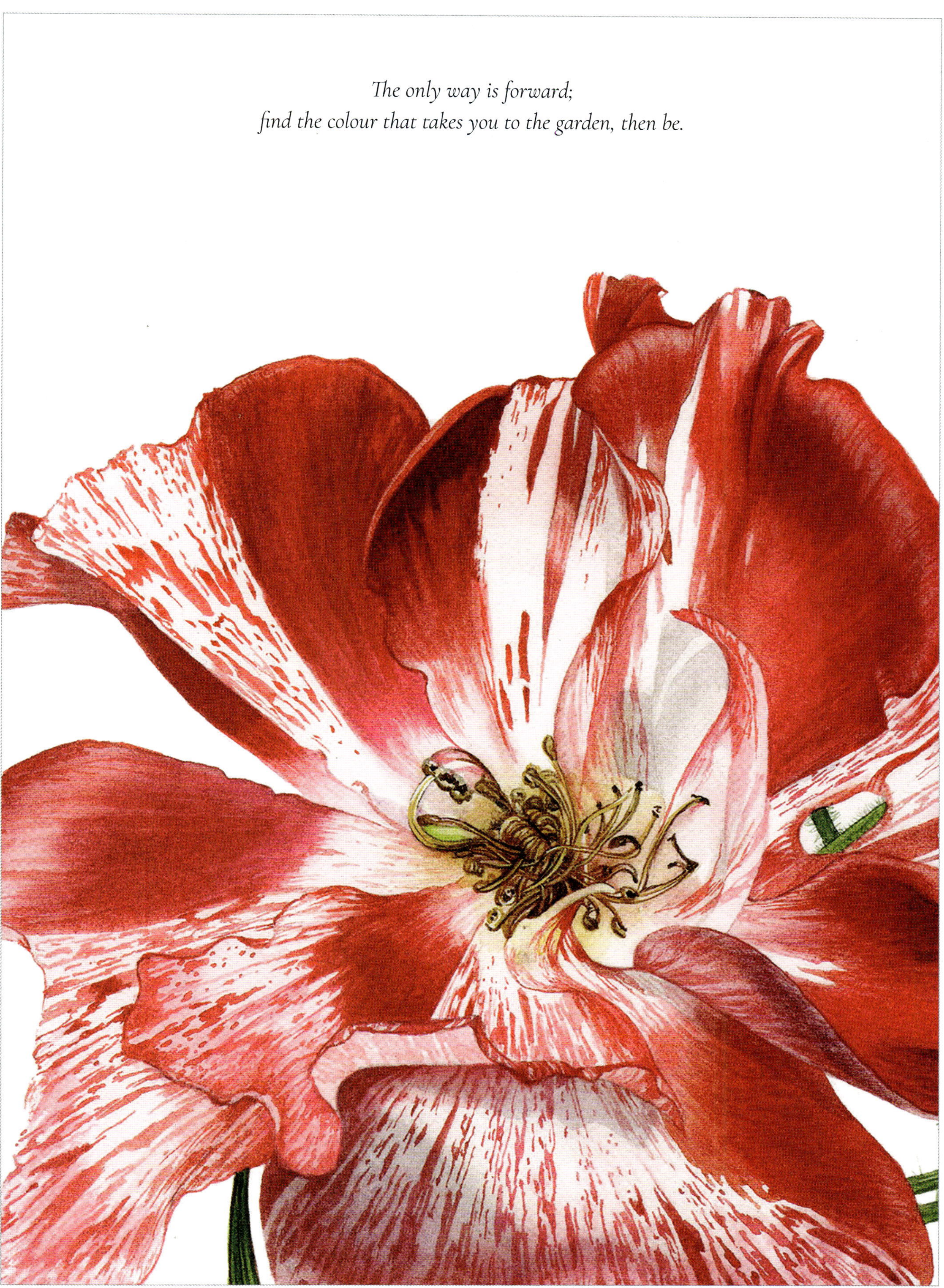

The only way is forward;
find the colour that takes you to the garden, then be.

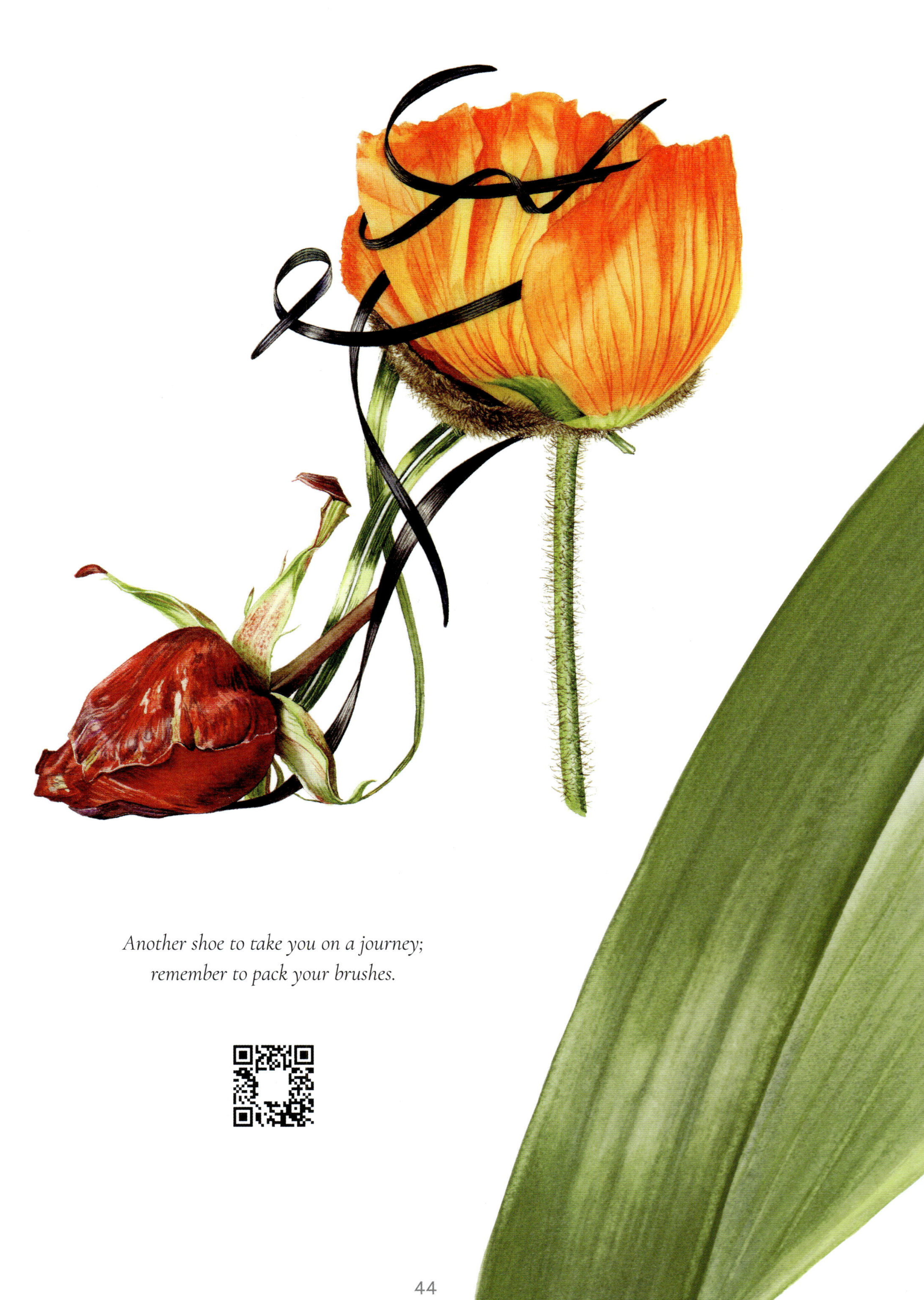

Another shoe to take you on a journey;
remember to pack your brushes.

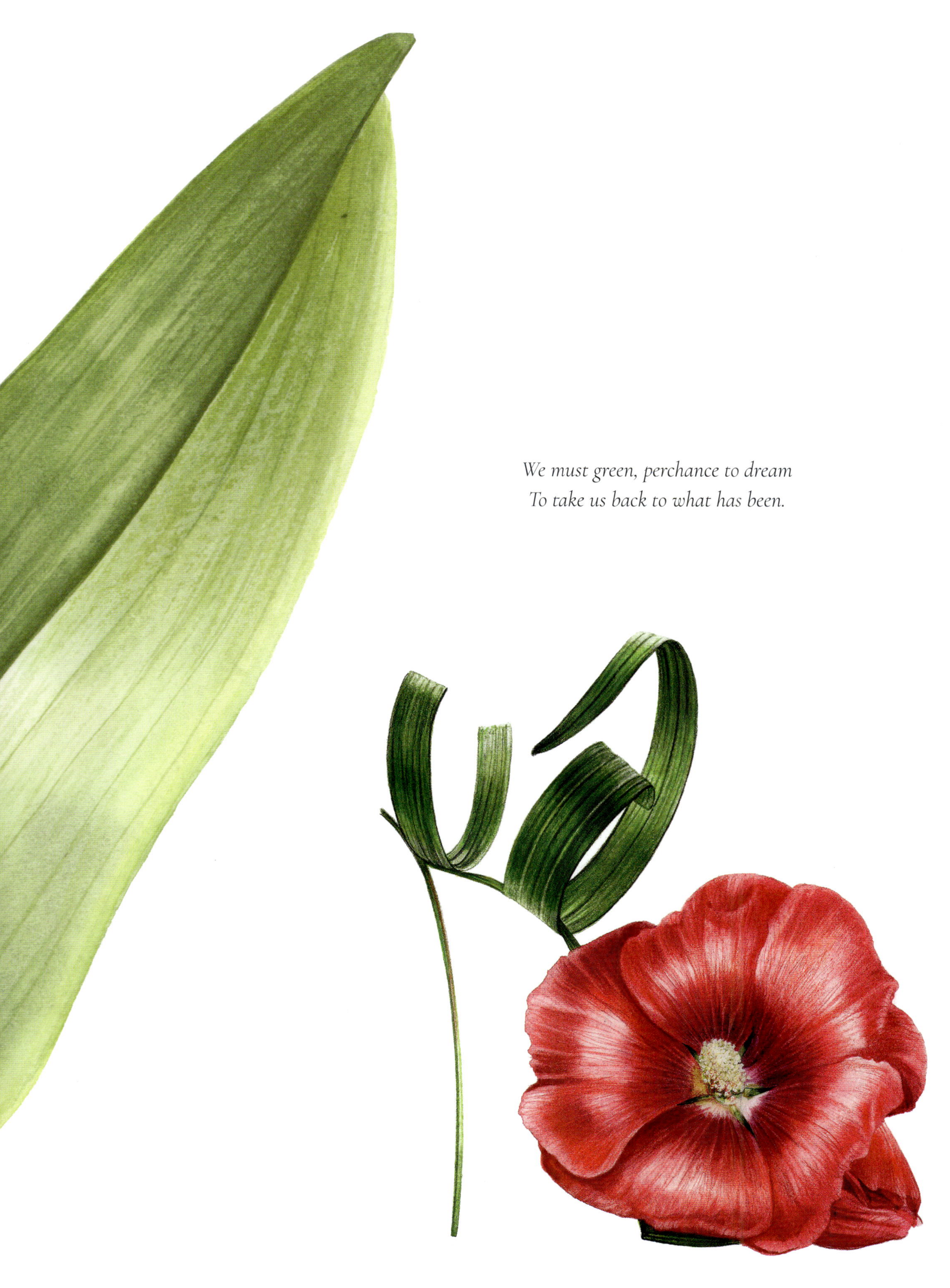

We must green, perchance to dream
To take us back to what has been.

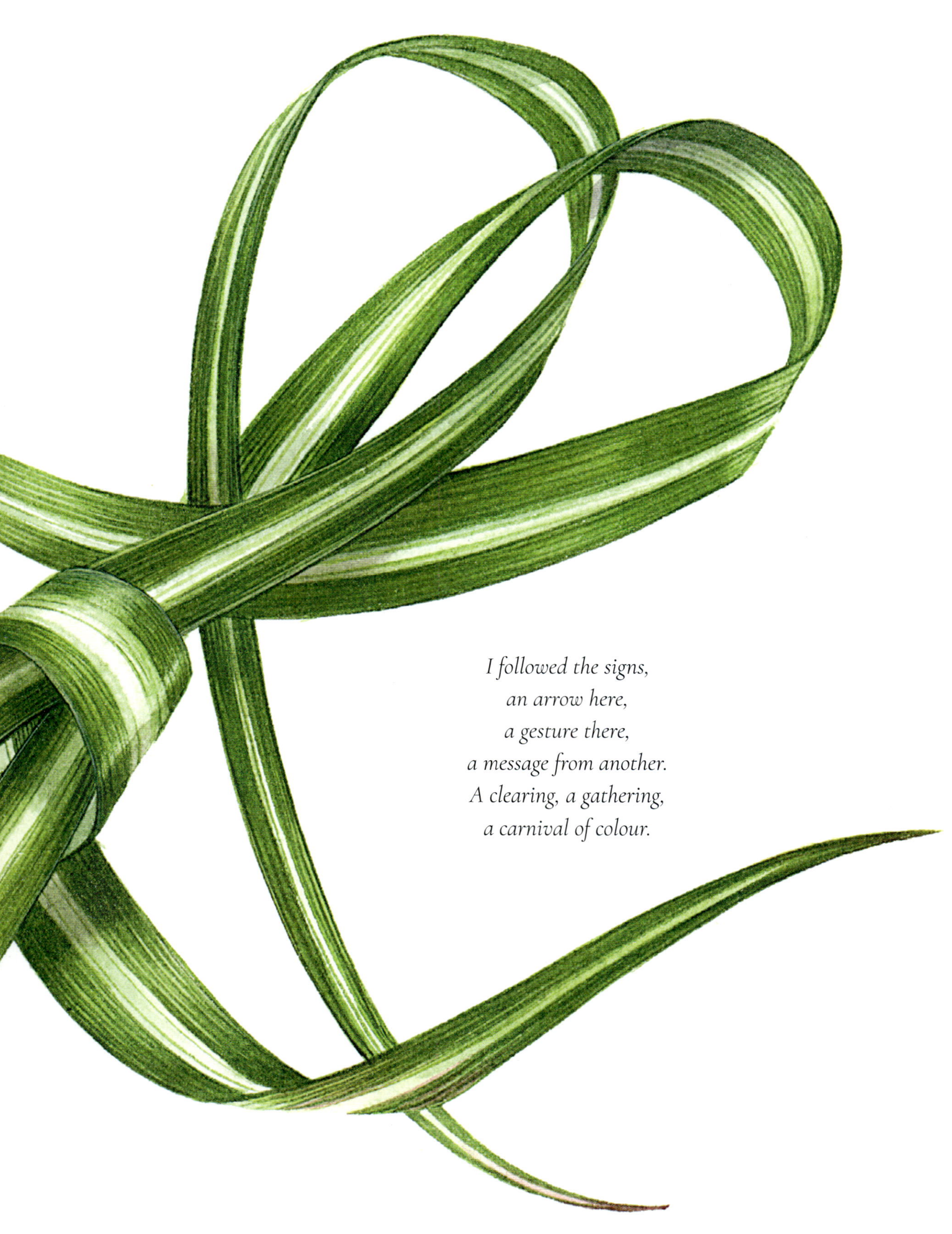

I followed the signs,
an arrow here,
a gesture there,
a message from another.
A clearing, a gathering,
a carnival of colour.

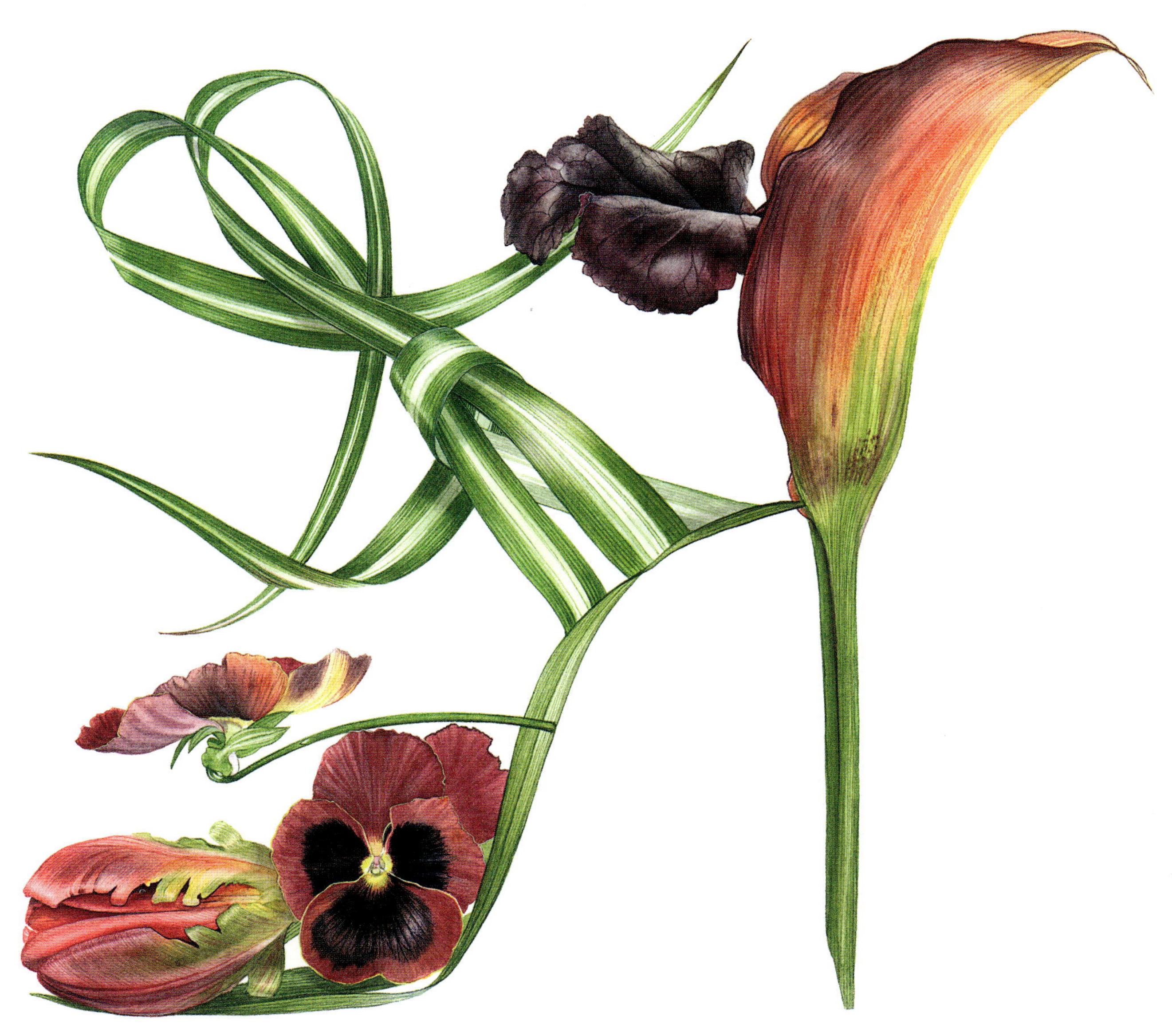

a *carnival*
of colour

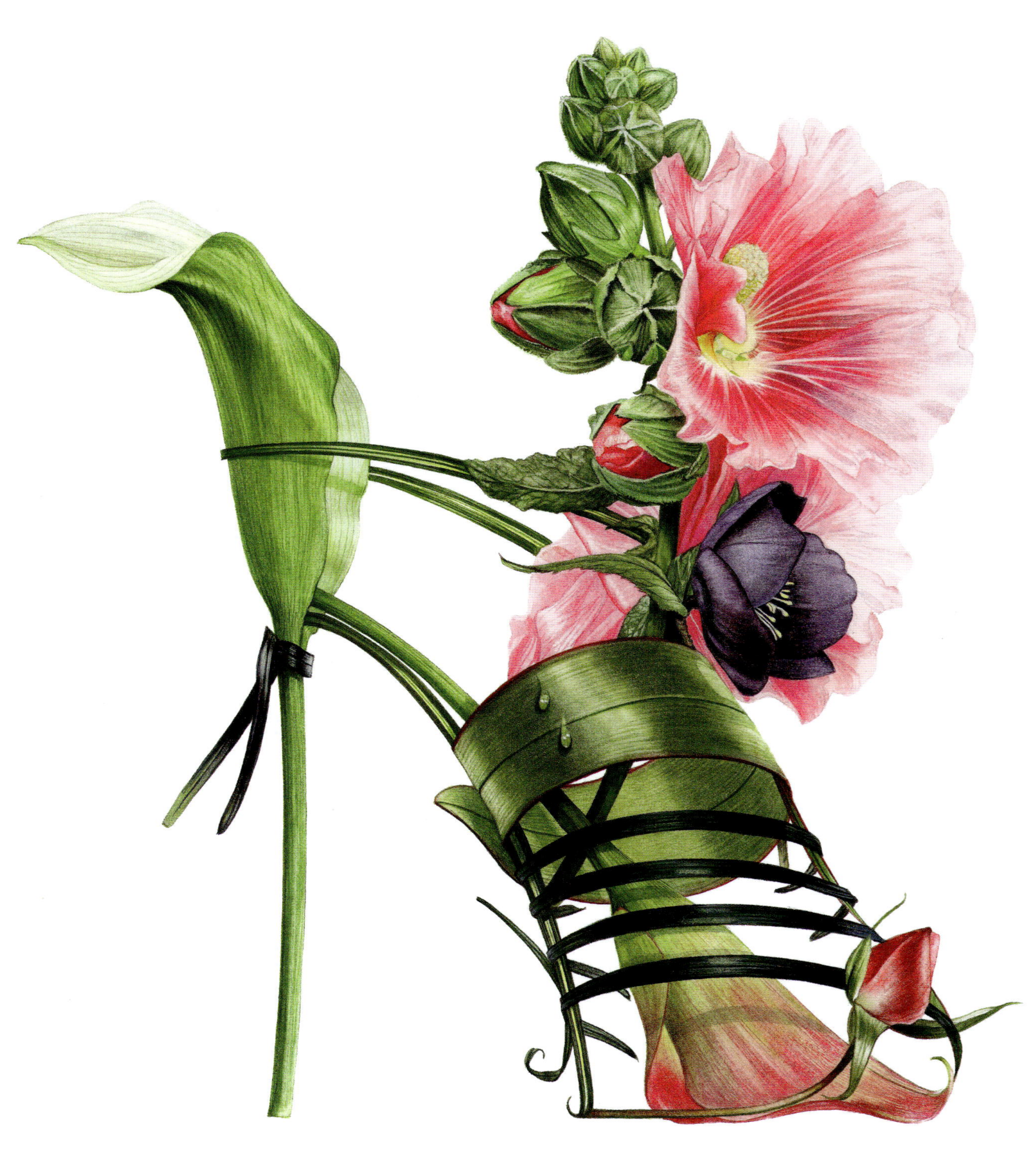

Every pair of shoes I have owned
have walked me to where I am today.

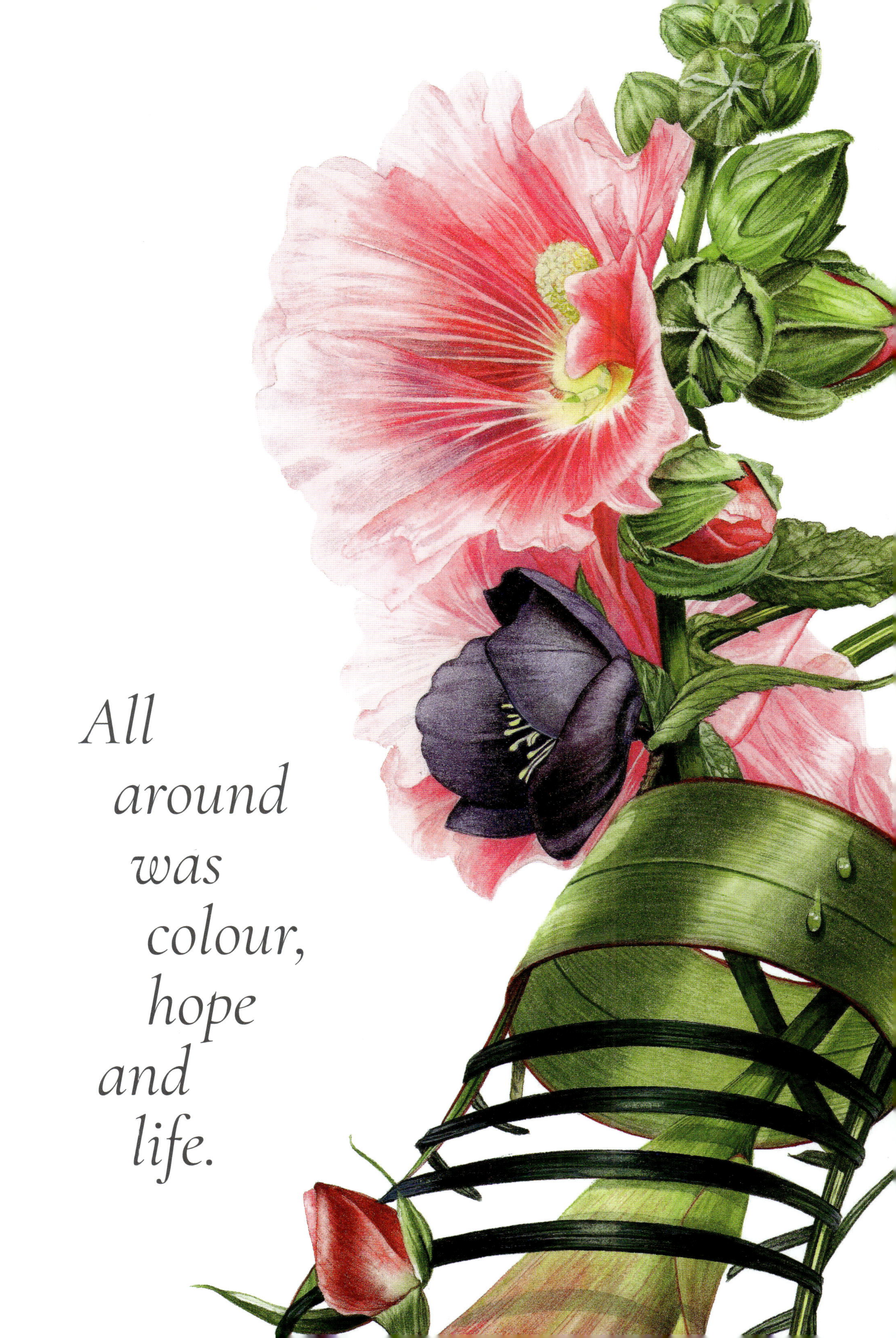
All
around
was
colour,
hope
and
life.

PINK

Be wary of pink; it comes with baggage.

Though one of my top colours of choice, I find that I battle with myself when selecting any pink bloom. How can a colour be haunted by gender when its splendour is beyond explanation?

Yes, it's romantic and yes, it is pretty but it is nearly always a colour of comfort, familiarity and subtlety in all its variations in hue.

Believe in pink, reclaim it from those that would dismiss it, and instead choose to wallow in its comforting glow.

For a strong pink, mix Helios purple and rose madder lake. For peachy pinks, add lemon to rose.

For the paler pinks, add water to any red and yet more water for the palest 'cherub sky' pink.

For the hottest pink, choose opera but enjoy it while you can.

The best pink of them all? Well, you choose.

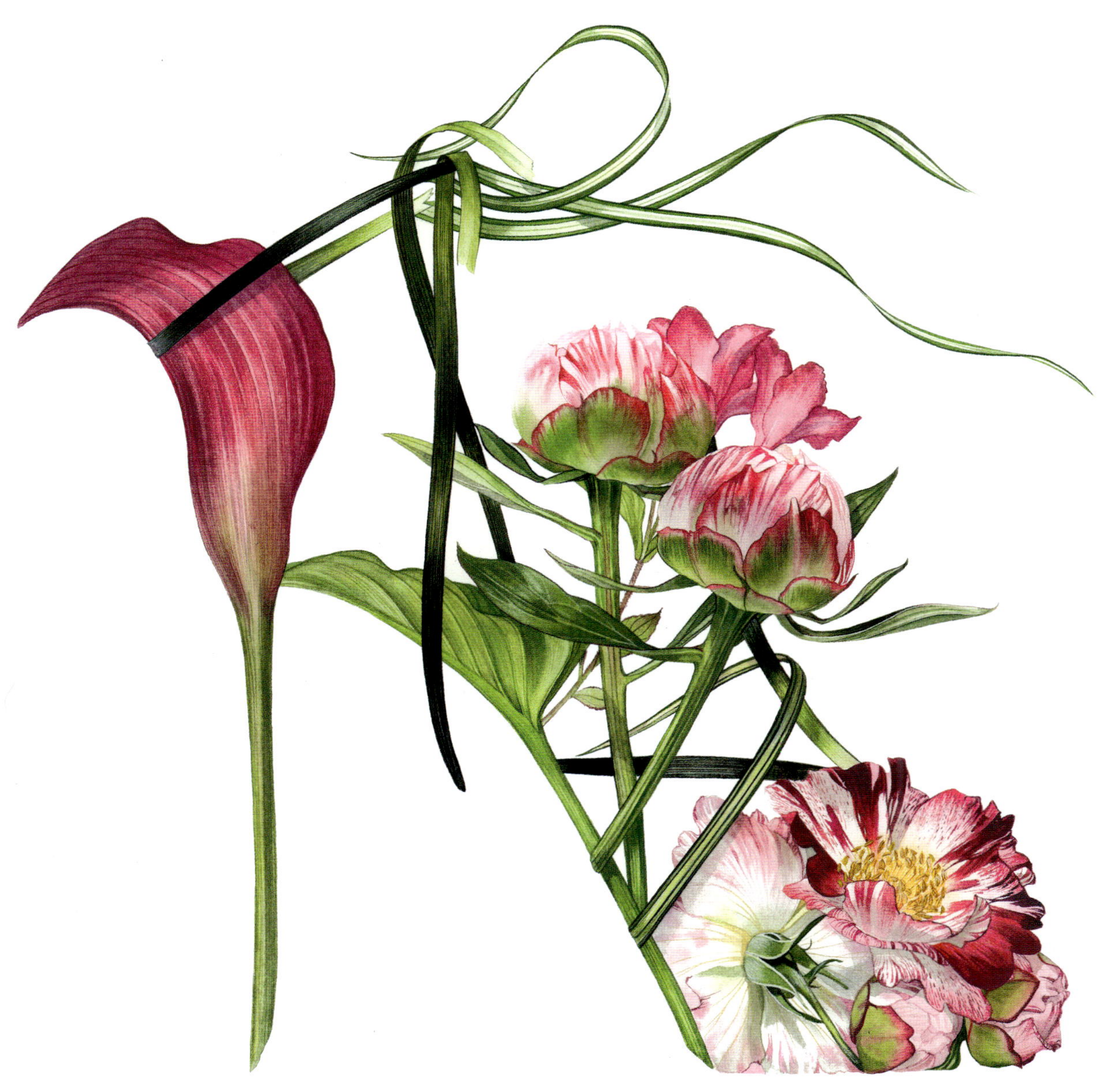

Splash of colour,
Dash of rose,
A silent skip.
A line of prose.
Travel in the morning
by call of larks and crows.

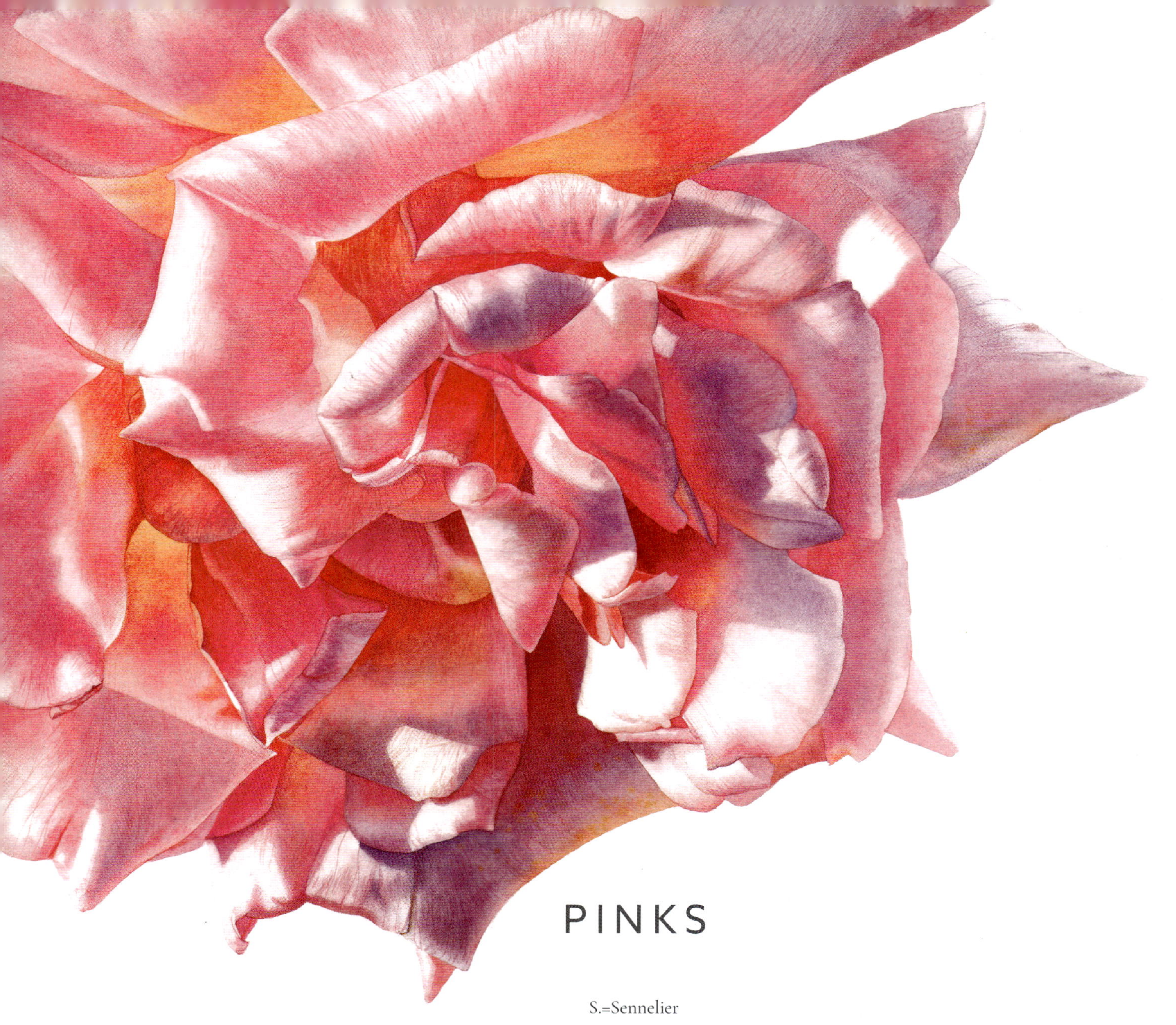

PINKS

S.=Sennelier

D.=Daniel Smith

COLUMN ONE

S. Quinacridone red

S. Quinacridone red + S. Rose madder

S. Quinacridone red + S. Rose madder + S. Helios purple

S. Quinacridone red + S. Rose madder + S. Helios purple +

S. Cobalt blue

S. Quinacridone red + S. Rose madder + S. Helios purple

S. Rose madder + S. Helios purple

S. Rose madder + S. Red orange

S. Quinacridone red + S. Helios purple

D. Quinacridone pink

COLUMN TWO

S. Quinacridone red + S. Lemon

S. Rose madder + S. Lemon

S. Rose madder + S. Lemon + S. Helios purple

S. Helios purple + S. Lemon

S. Red orange + S. Rose madder

S. Rose madder + S. Red orange + S. Helios purple

S. Rose madder + S. Yellow deep + D. Quinacridone pink

S. Helios purple + S. Lemon + D. Quinacridone pink

S. Helios purple + S. Rose madder

Baby girl

Baby boy

Cotton pink

Sugar almond pink

Candy cup

Cherish

Blossom heart

Blusher

Maiden rose

Fuchsia veil

Regal dream

Sweet heart

Happy heart

Mother flame

Fresh pudding pink

Syrup red

Sweet cherry

Obsession

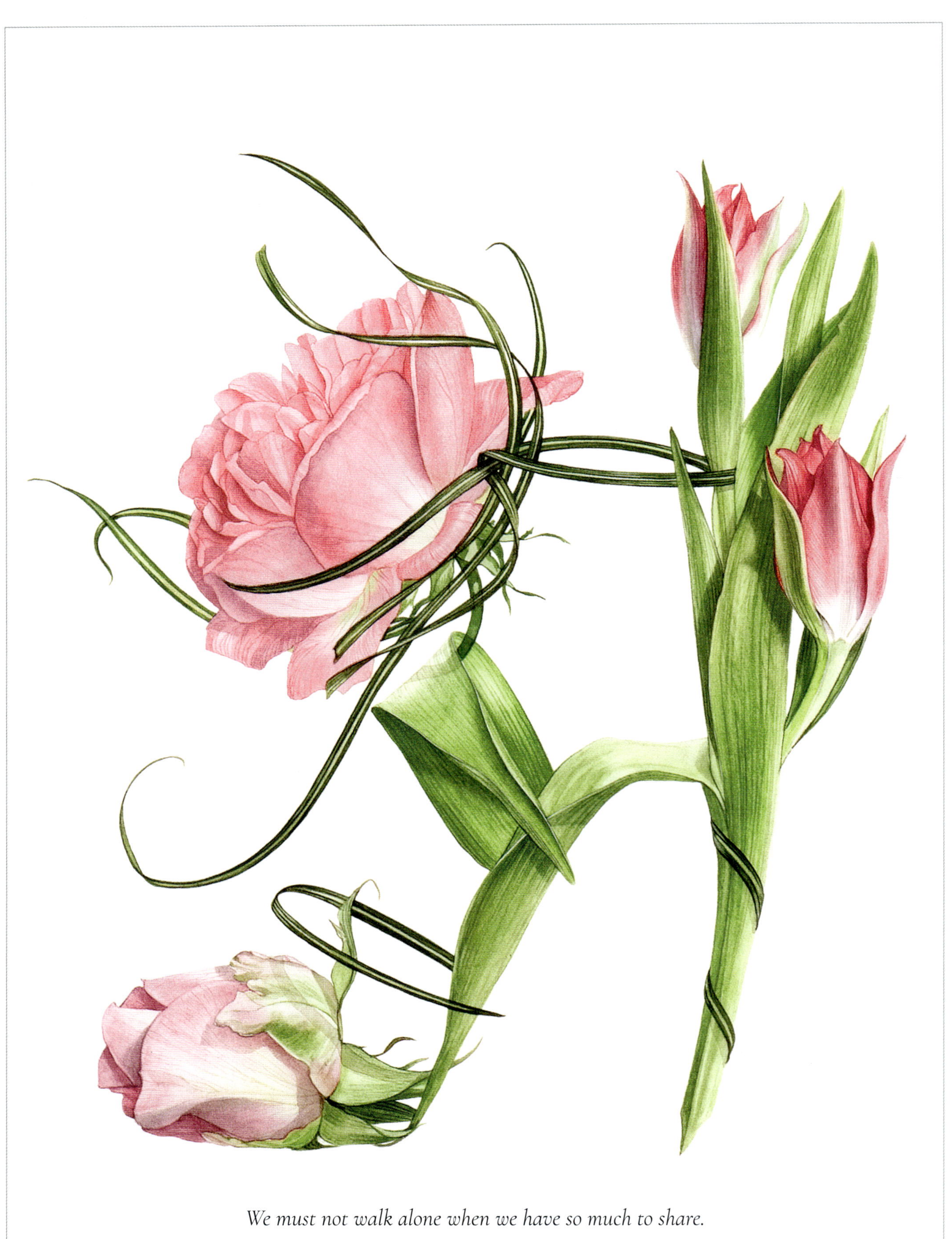

We must not walk alone when we have so much to share.

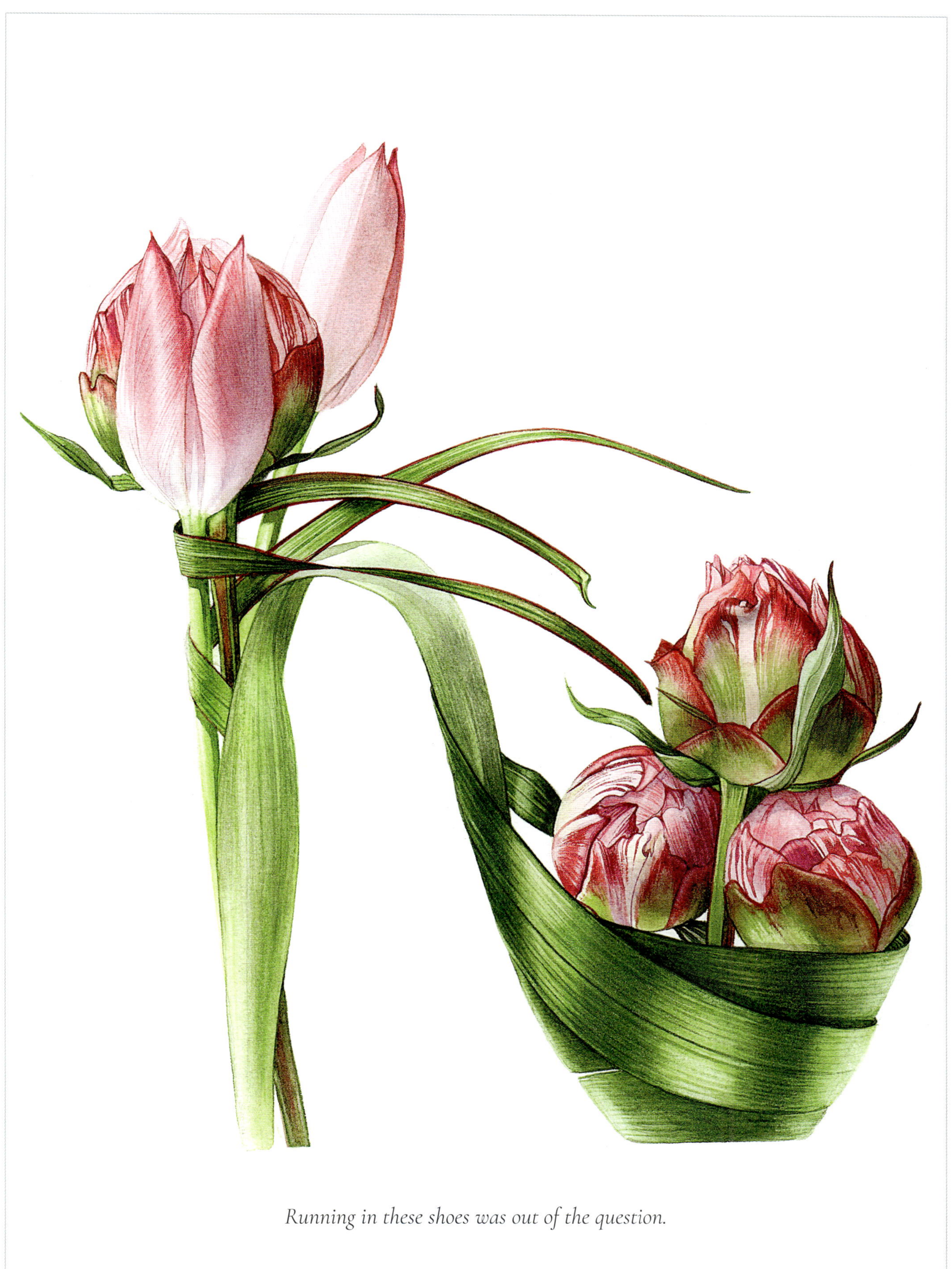

Running in these shoes was out of the question.

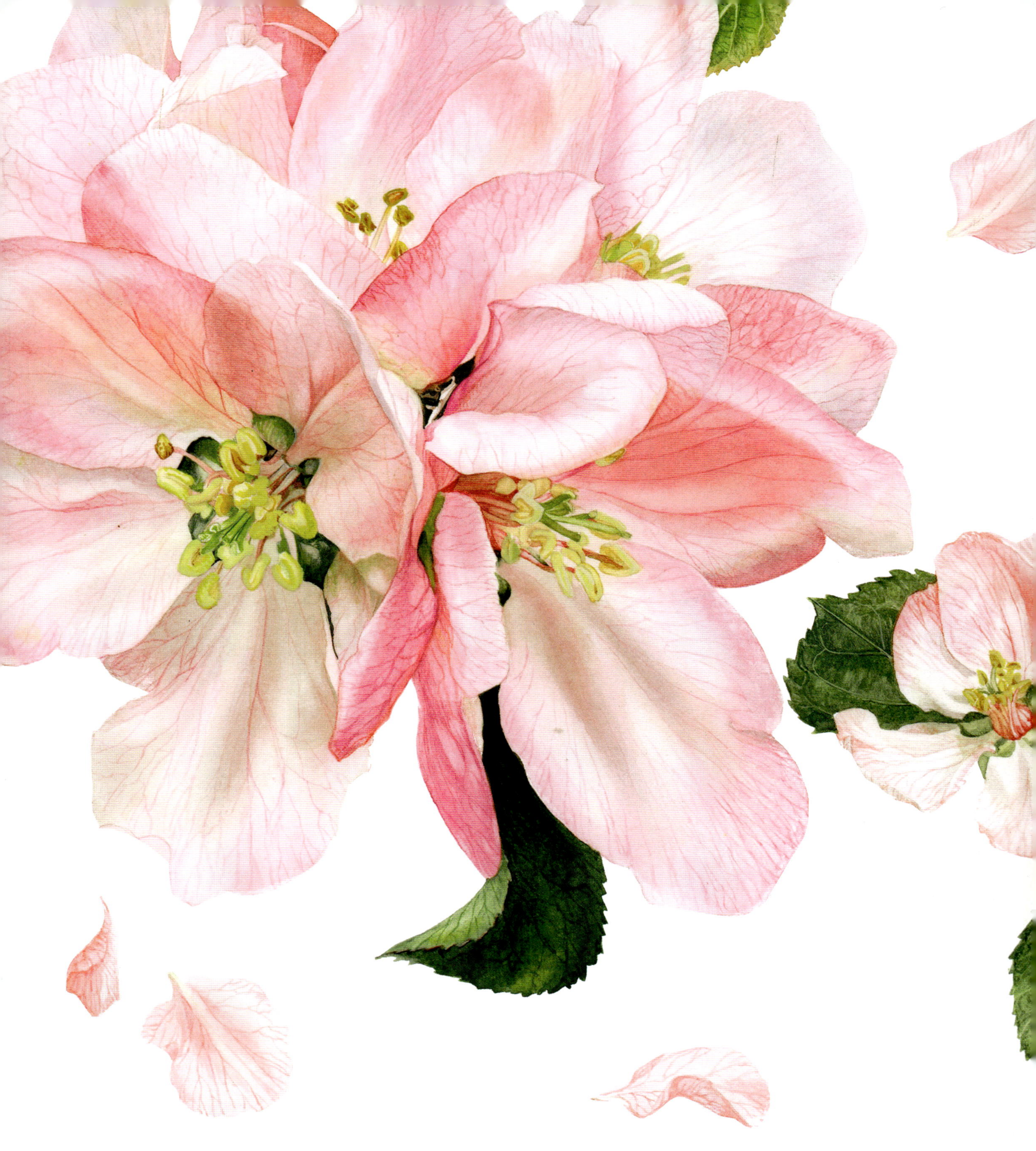

Your journey will take you beneath scented boughs,
Your path can be traced through a tumble of flowers.
This colour will fill all the beautiful hours.

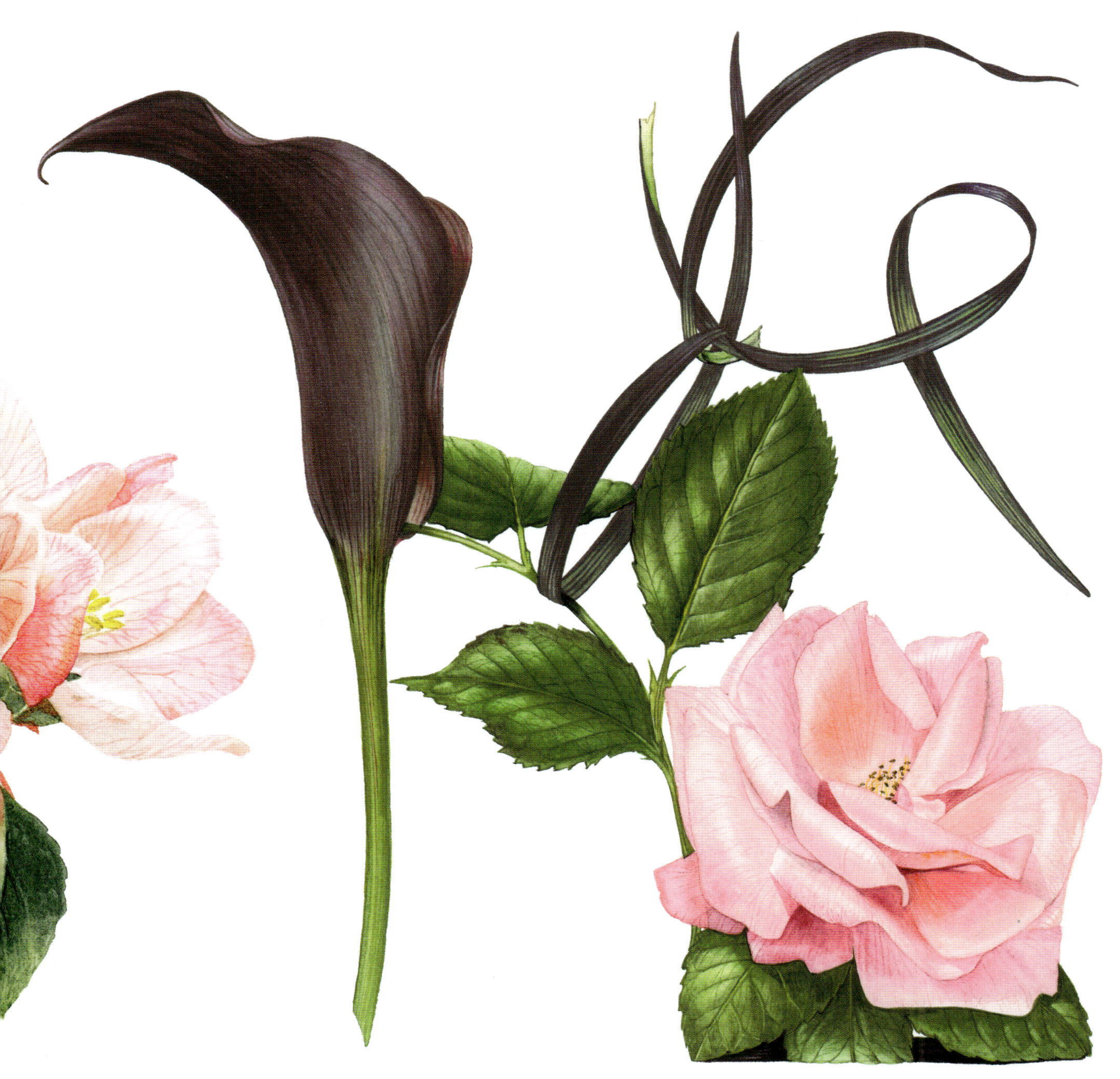

The road is behind you, the path is afore.
The signs led you far from the journey's beginning.
Every step is questioned,
Yet every decision made along the way,
Curiously carries you forward.

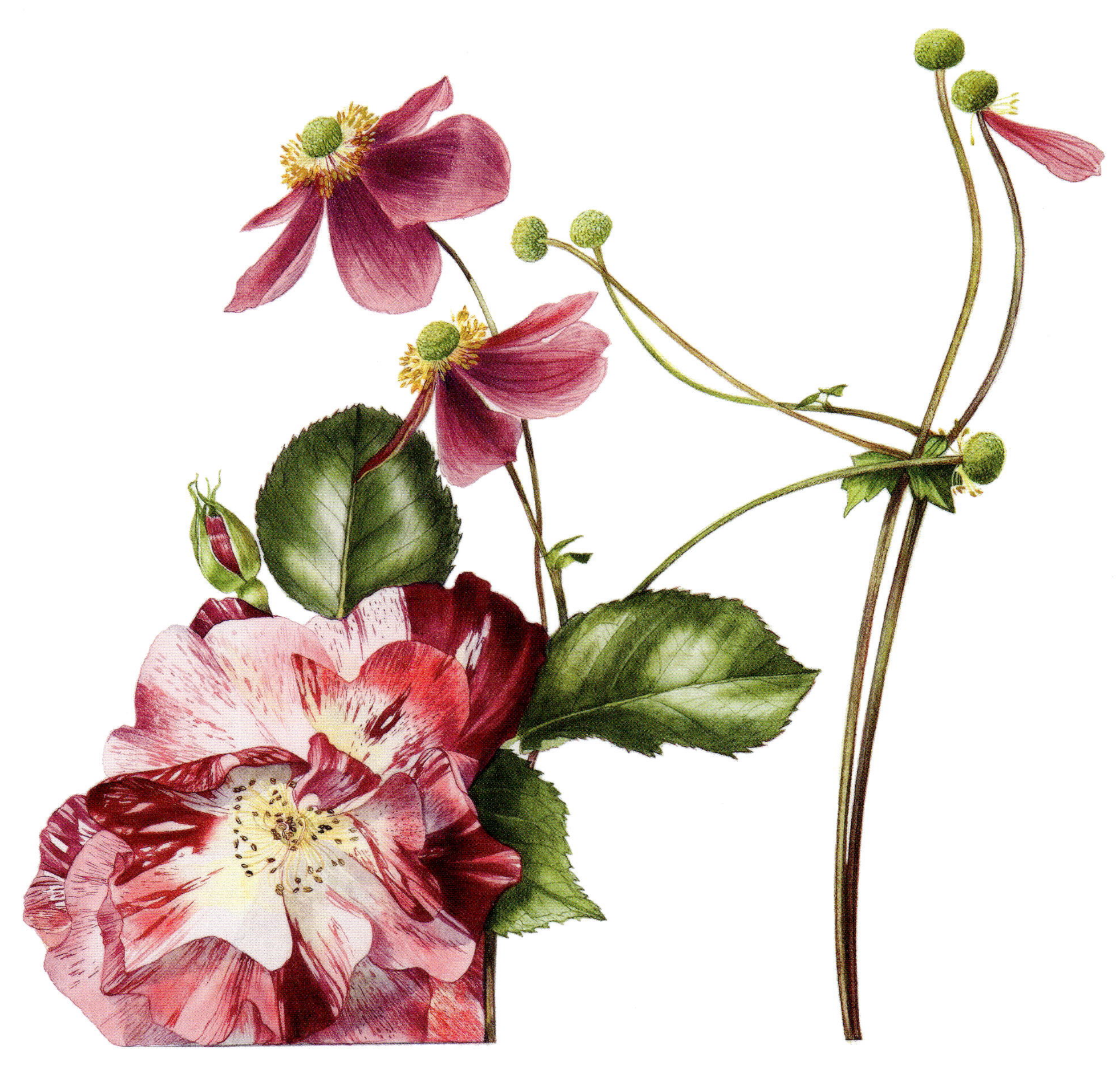

I am here beneath the fallen petals, keeping calm
Remaining small.
'Til all is quiet,
I won't come out at all.

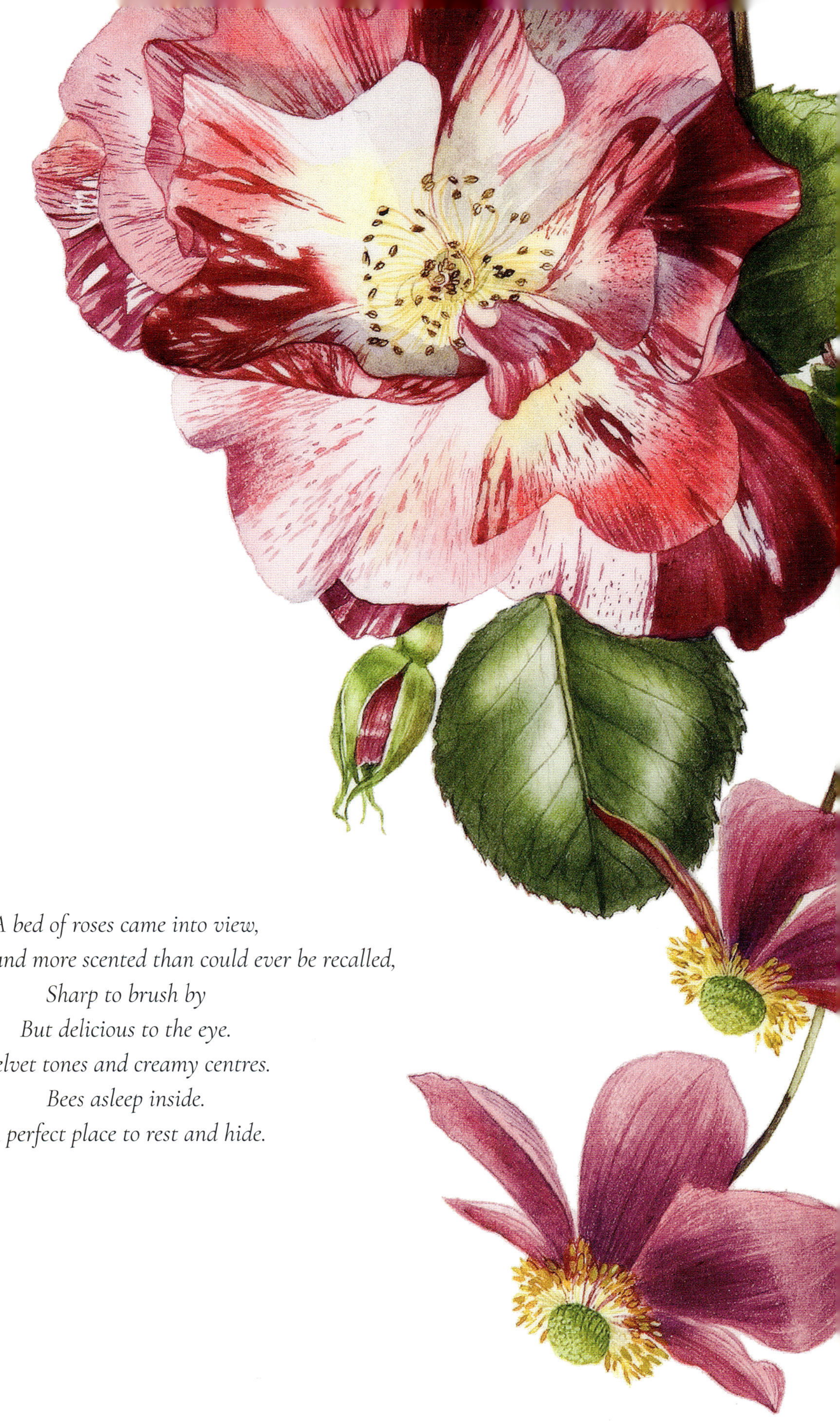

A bed of roses came into view,
More colourful and more scented than could ever be recalled,
Sharp to brush by
But delicious to the eye.
Velvet tones and creamy centres.
Bees asleep inside.
A perfect place to rest and hide.

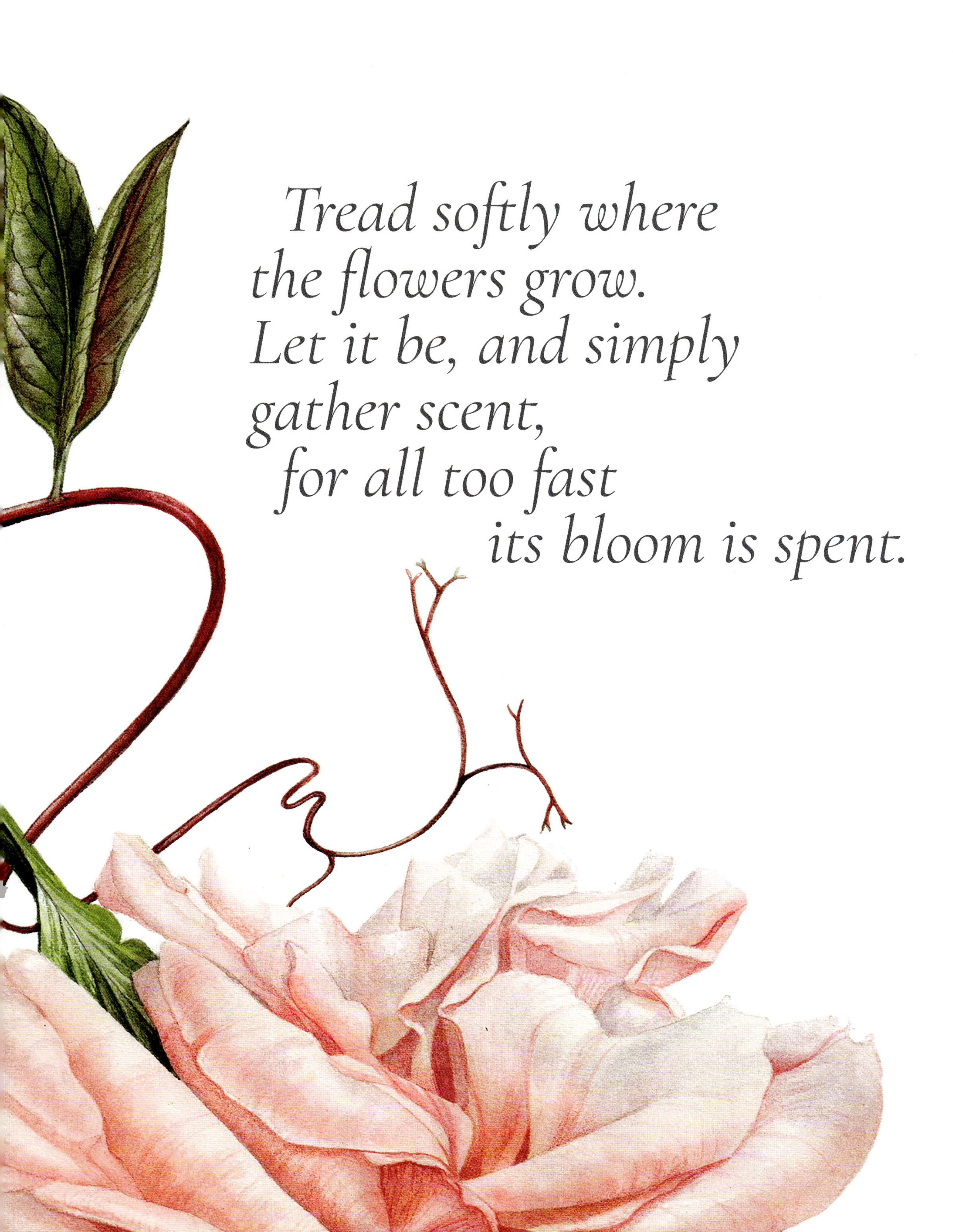

Tread softly where
the flowers grow.
Let it be, and simply
gather scent,
for all too fast
its bloom is spent.

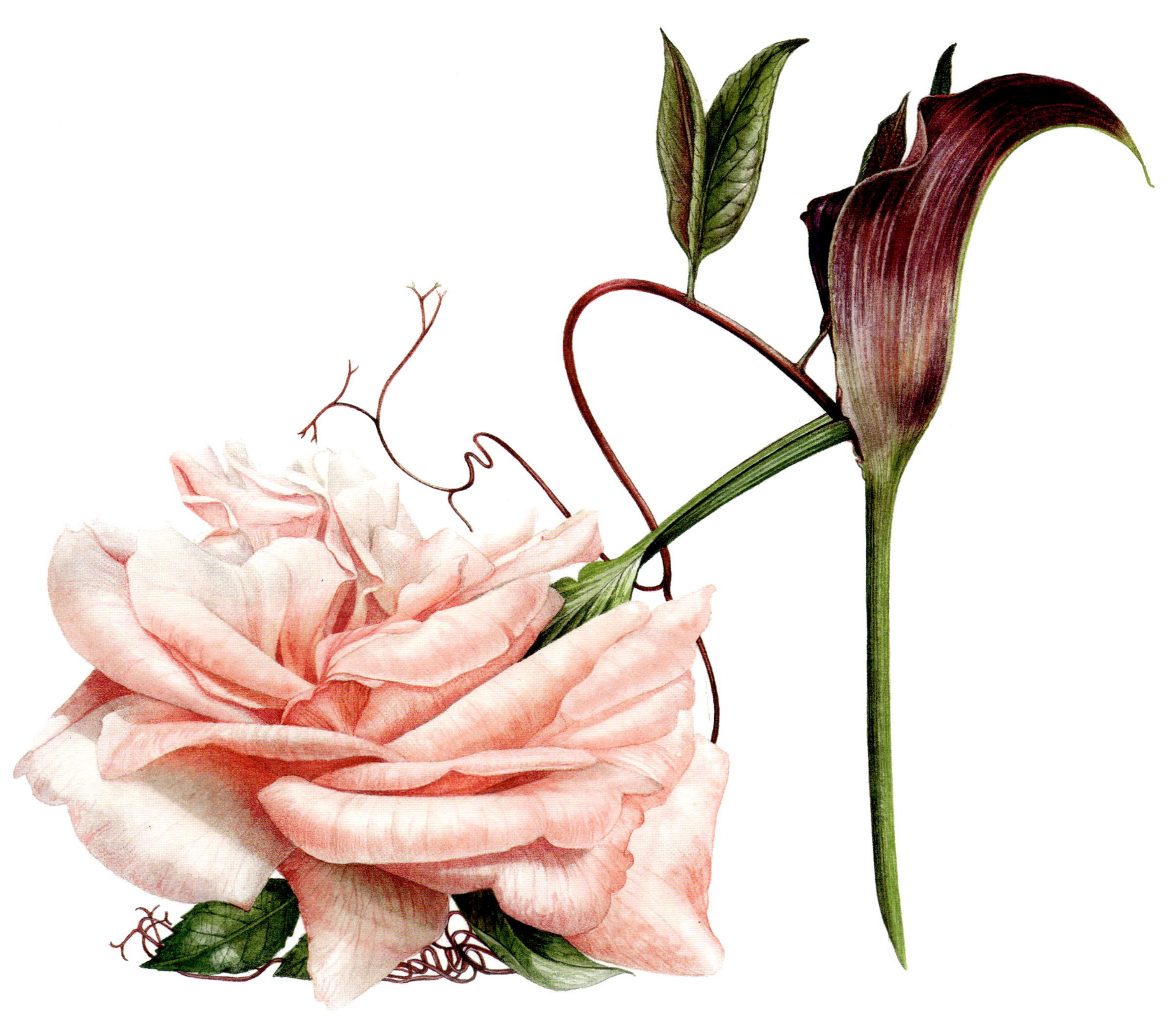

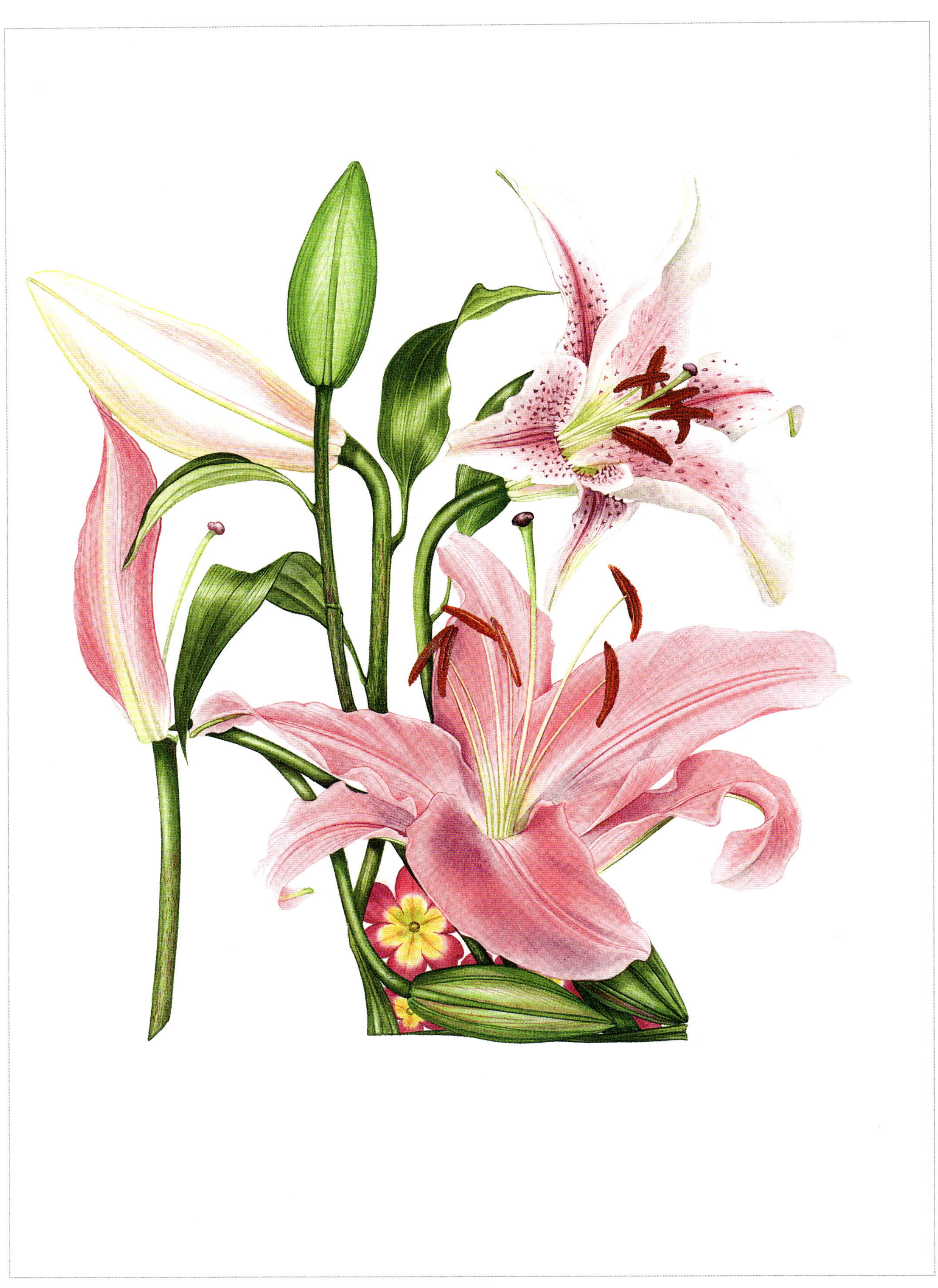

DREAM PREMONITION

We will meet along the way
We won't be prepared.
It will be a sign,
Our destiny is shared.
Perfect pink will be the tint
For this was meant to be.
Obsession pink for you,
And maiden rose for me.

BLUE LILAC

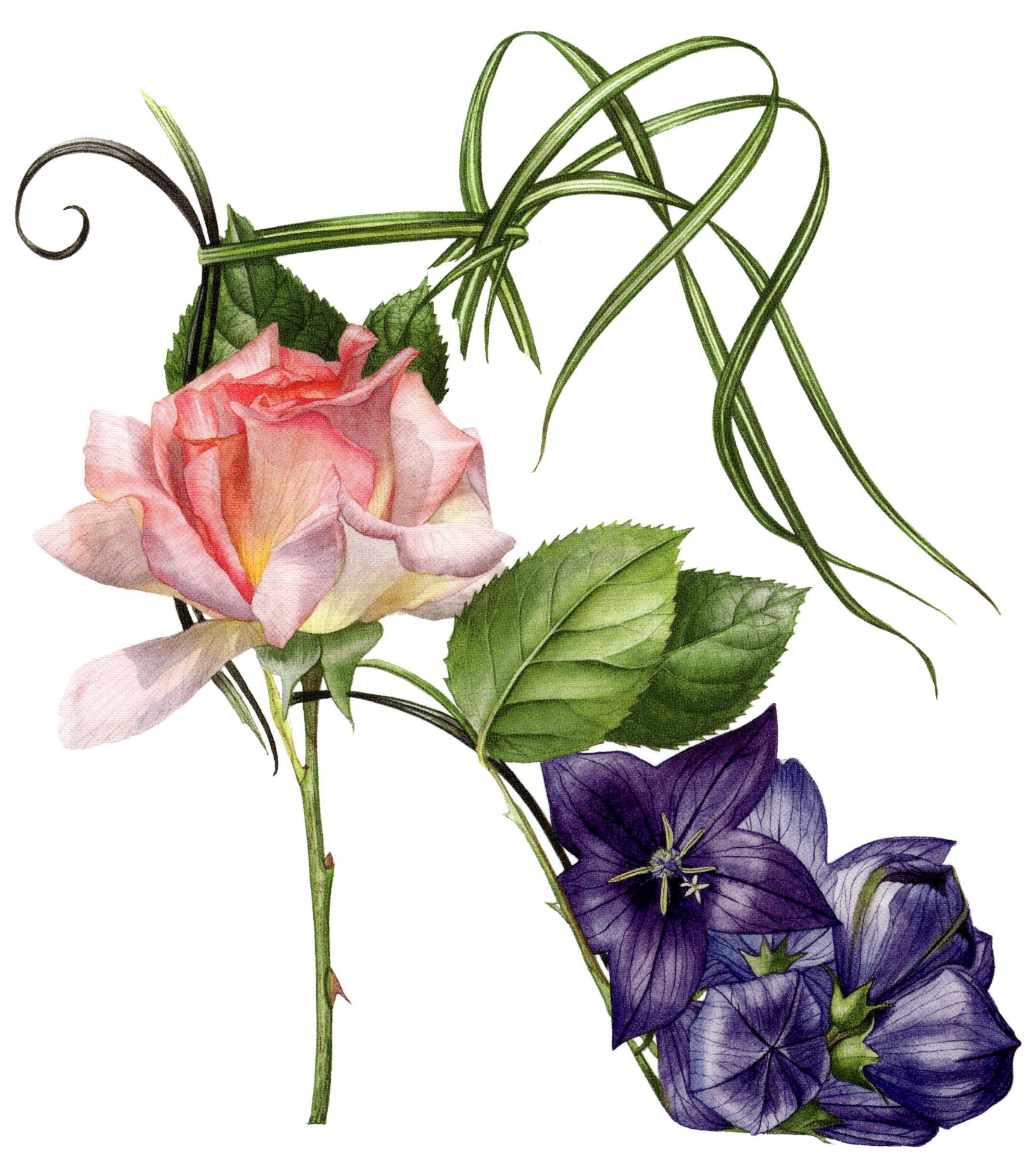

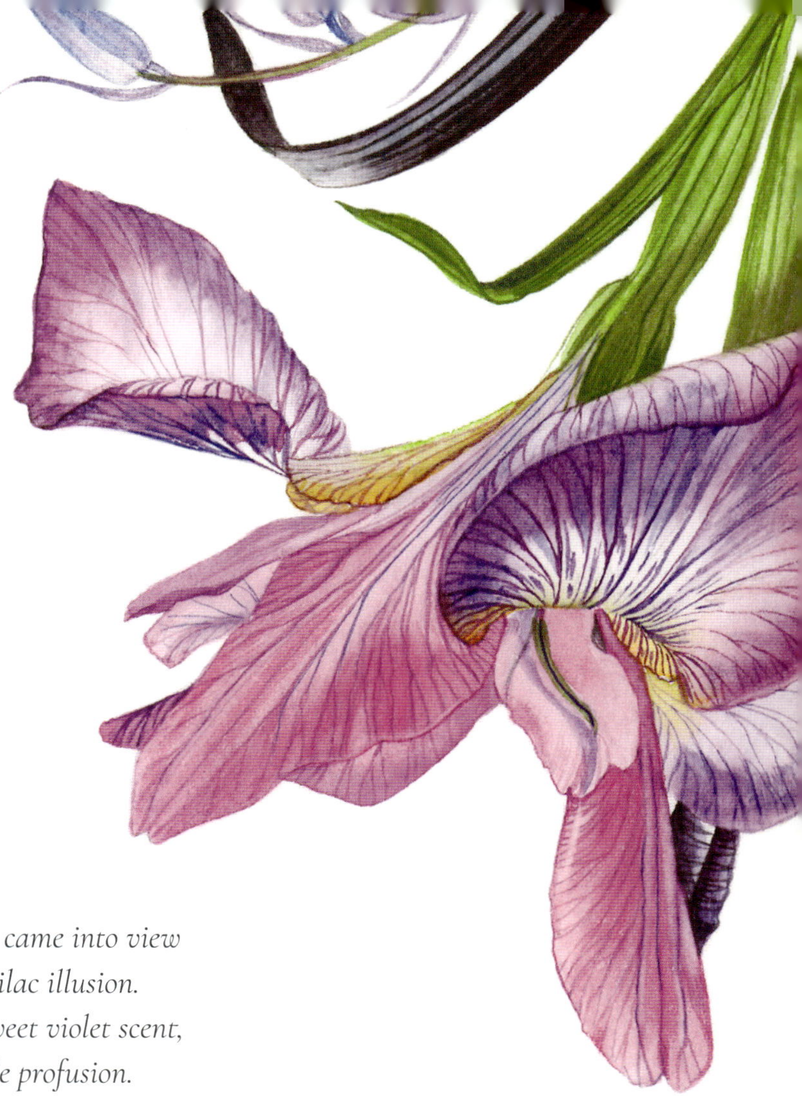

A morning vision came into view
A veiled and lilac illusion.
A spirit dream, sweet violet scent,
Of perfect pale profusion.
The early dawn left us adrift
In heaven's landscape dream.
We came to rest in purple pool
Then vanished from the scene.

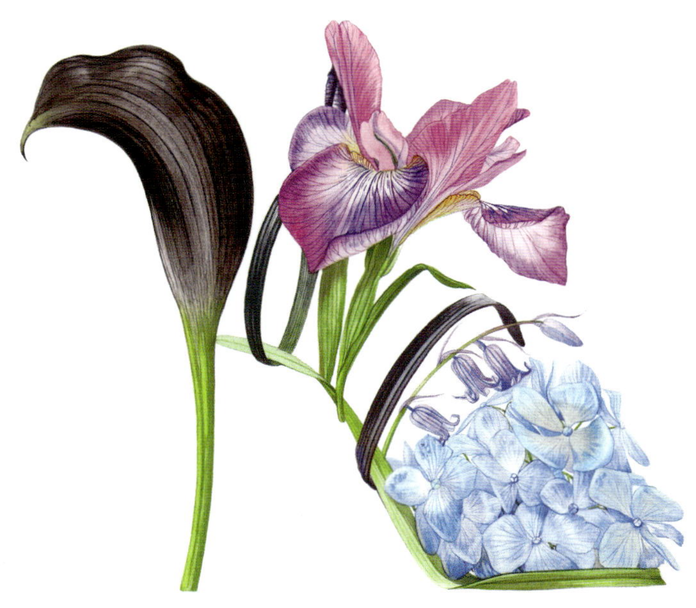

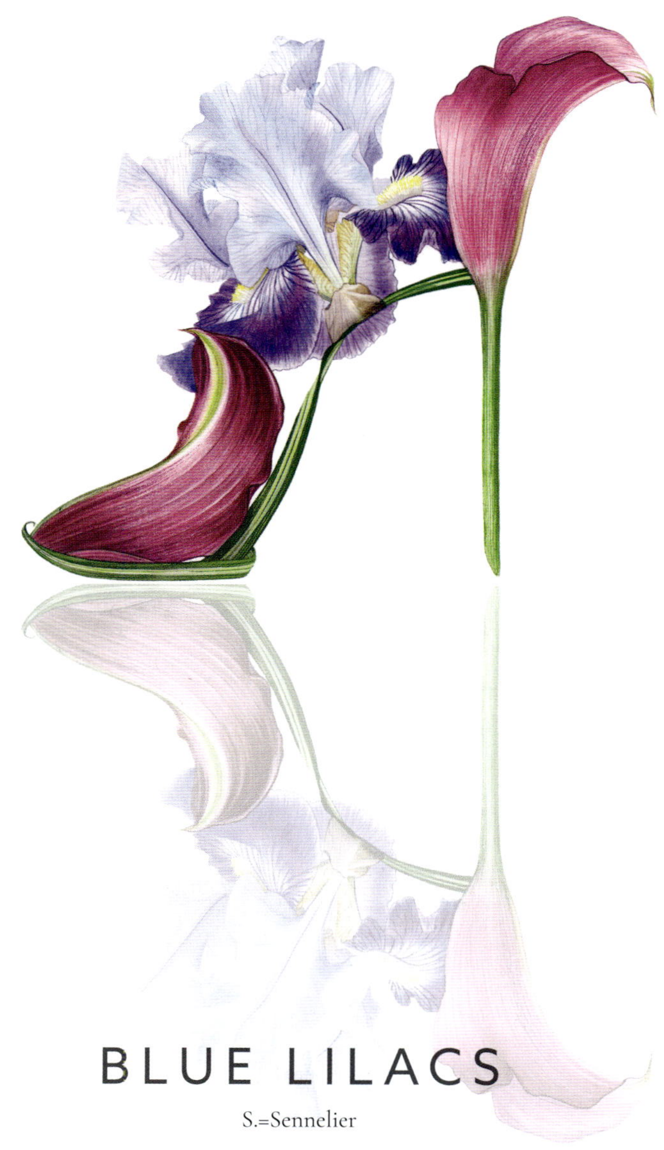

BLUE LILACS

S.=Sennelier

COLUMN ONE

S. Blue violet

S. Blue violet + S. Cobalt blue

S. Blue violet + S. French ultramarine

S. Dioxazine purple + S. Cobalt blue

S. Dioxazine purple + S. French ultramarine

S. Dioxazine purple + S. Indigo

S. Dioxazine purple + S. Indigo + S. French ultramarine

S. Blue violet + S. Dioxazine purple

S. Blue violet + S. Dioxazine purple + S. French ultramarine

COLUMN TWO

S. Blue violet + S. Quinacridone red

S. Helios purple + S. Cobalt blue

S. Helios purple + S. Cobalt blue + S. French ultramarine

S. Helios purple + S. Blue violet

S. Helios purple + S. Dioxazine purple

S. Rose madder + S. Cobalt blue

S. Rose madder + S. French ultramarine

S. Rose madder + S. French ultramarine + S. Yellow deep

S. Helios purple + S. Dioxazine purple + S. Yellow deep

COLUMN ONE	COLUMN TWO
Morning vision	*Sweet violet rose*
Veiled illusion	*Veiled rose*
Spirit dream	*Violet cream*
Sweet violet	*Sugared violets*
Pale profusion	*Violet glove*
Early dawn	*Opulence*
Adrift	*Raspberry violet*
Purple pool	*Blue violet syrup*
Royal velvet	*Plum violet*

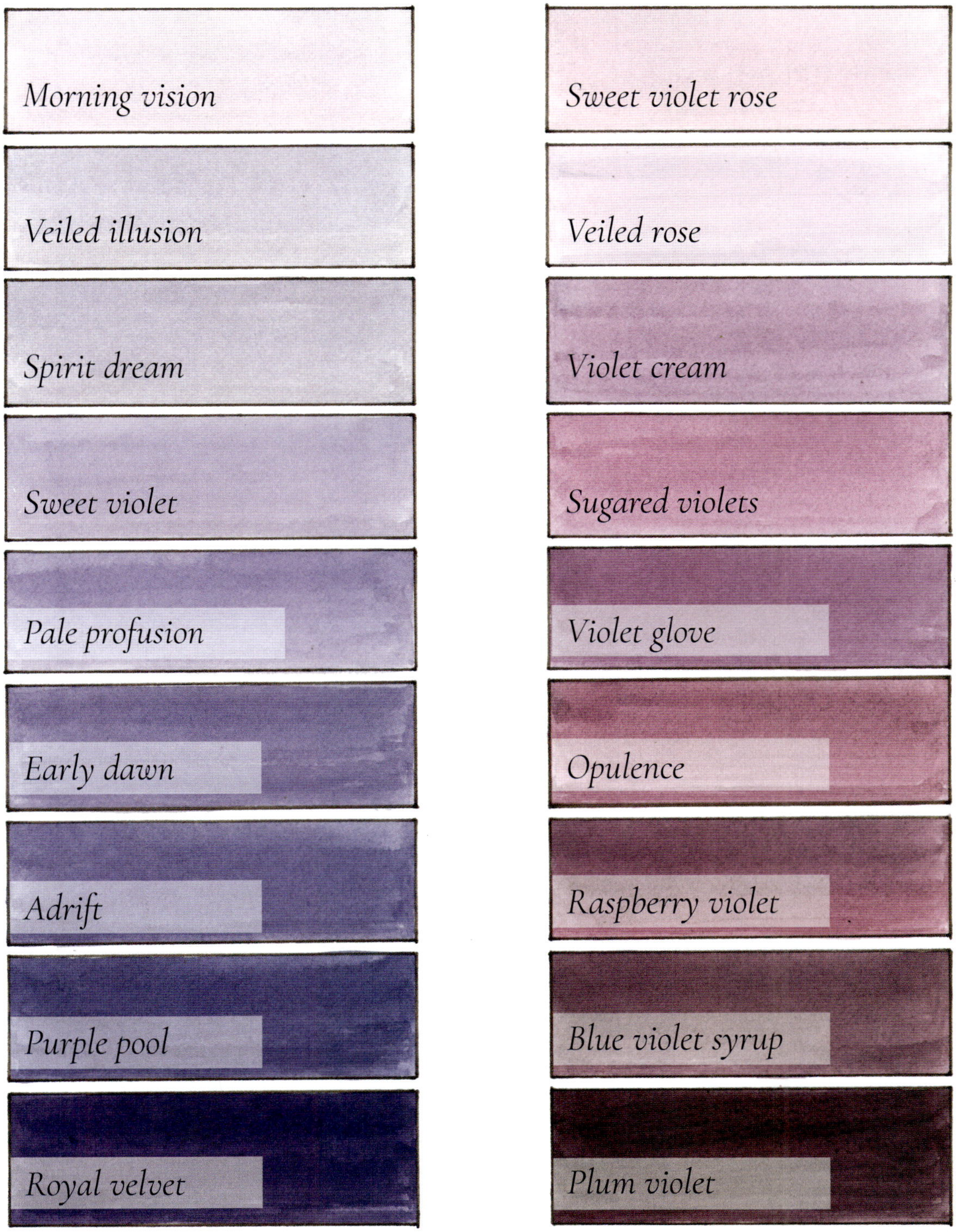

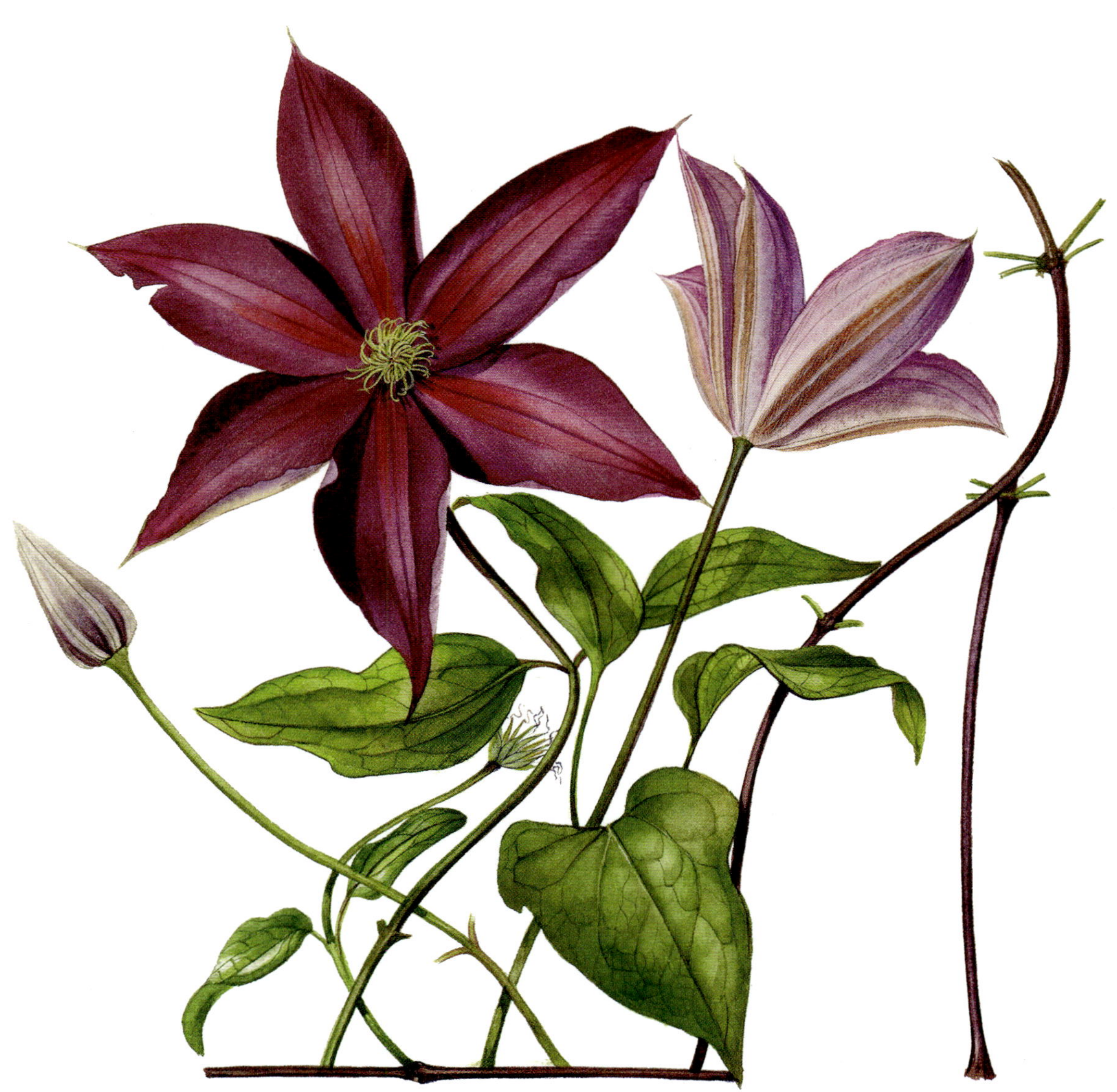

Lilacs and purples are the royalty of the garden and palette, with so many possible variations. Even muddy purples make the grade. In nature, purple is frequently paired with yellow and they can bring out the best in each other. When they collide, a beautiful chocolate purple can often emerge from the union. See my colours 'Blue violet syrup' and 'Plum violet': both have small amounts of yellow in the mix.

Play with your colours. Put out a pure pigment and add a small amount of another colour. Mix it strong or water it down and then note what happens and how the colour makes you feel. Soon you will be mixing all the colours from the garden.

The meadow is magical, shining, sublime
The leaves grow tall, so tapered and fine.
Caressing in shapes as they start to climb,
Inspiring to make the perfect design.

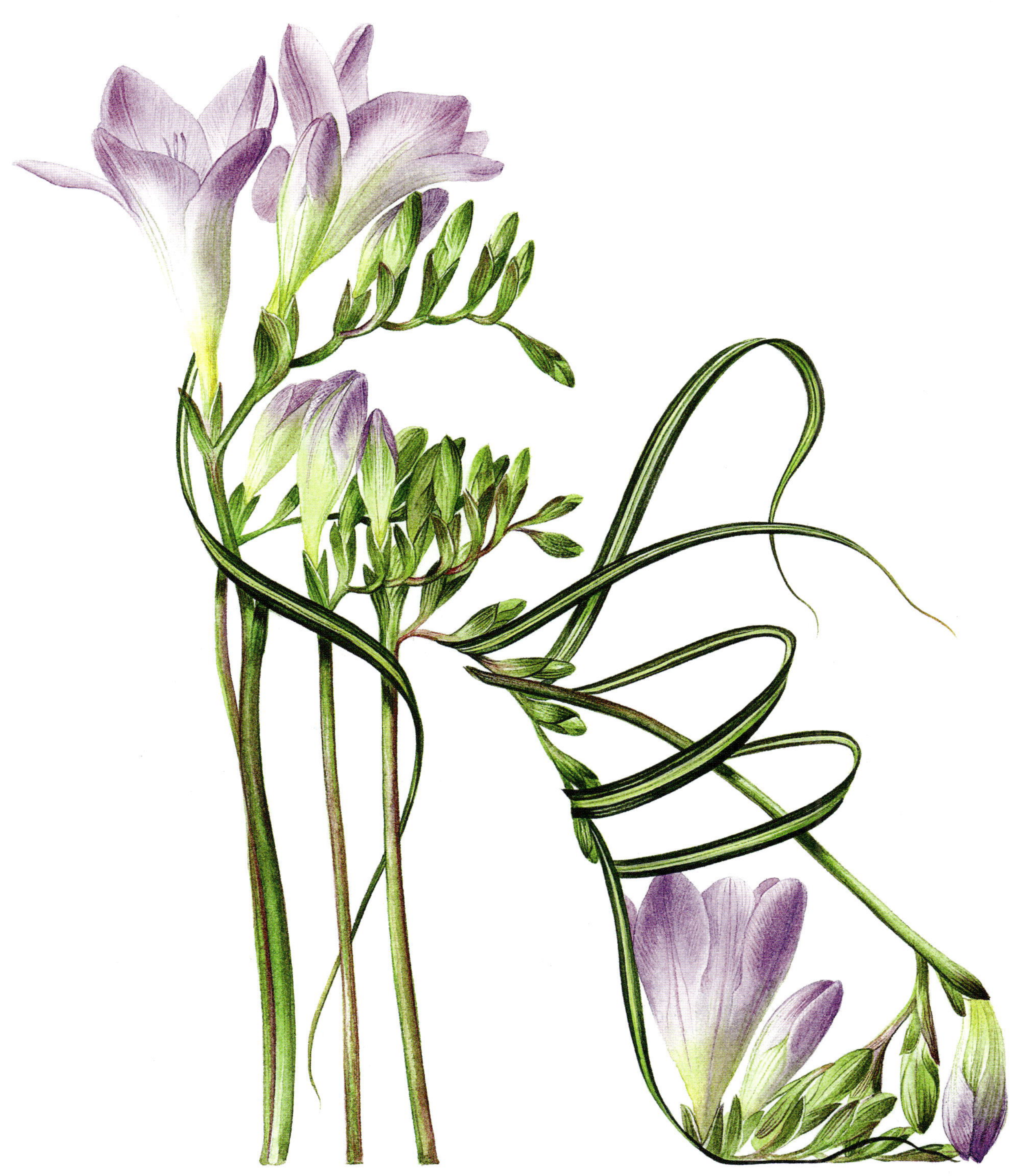

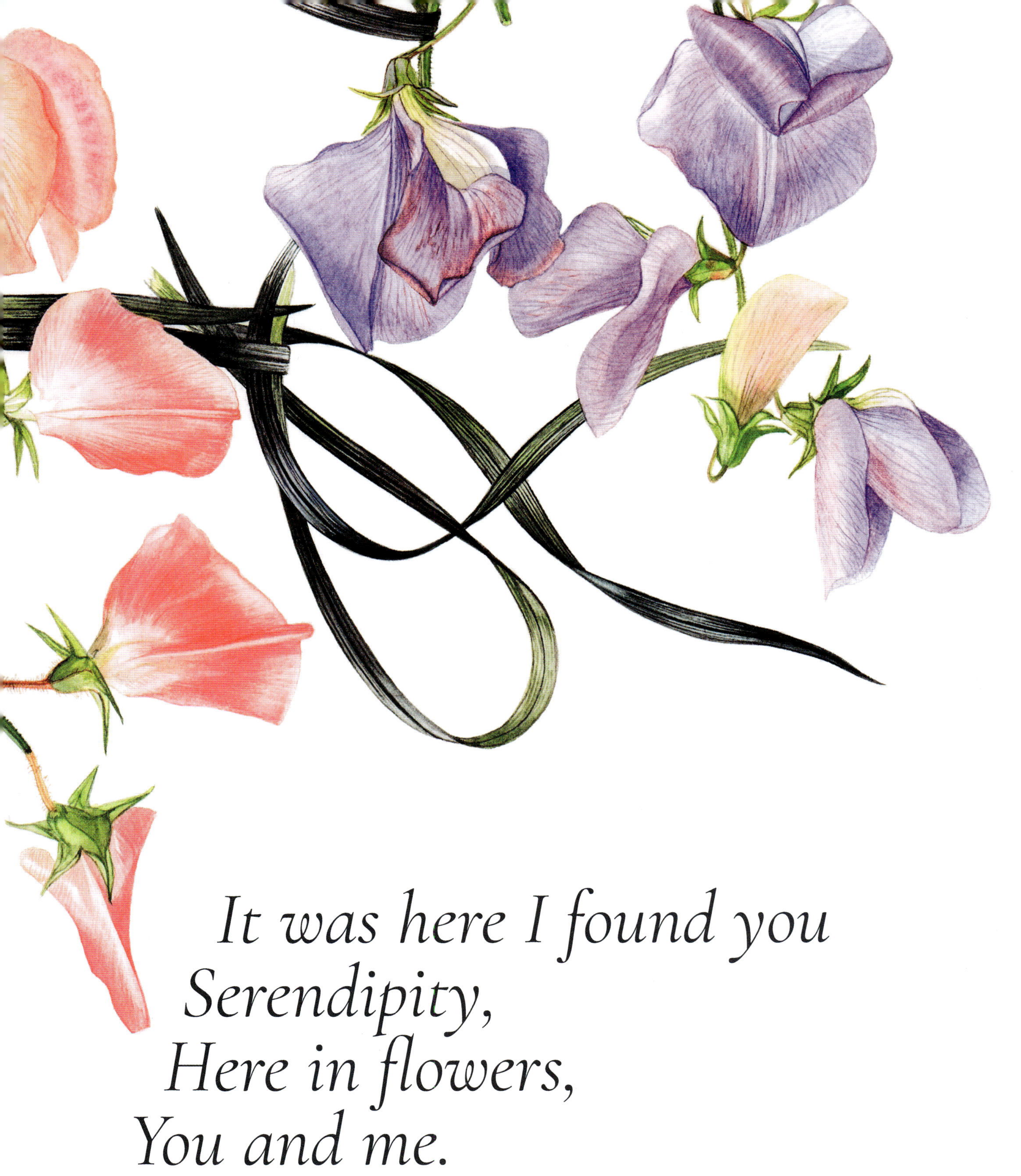

It was here I found you
Serendipity,
Here in flowers,
You and me.

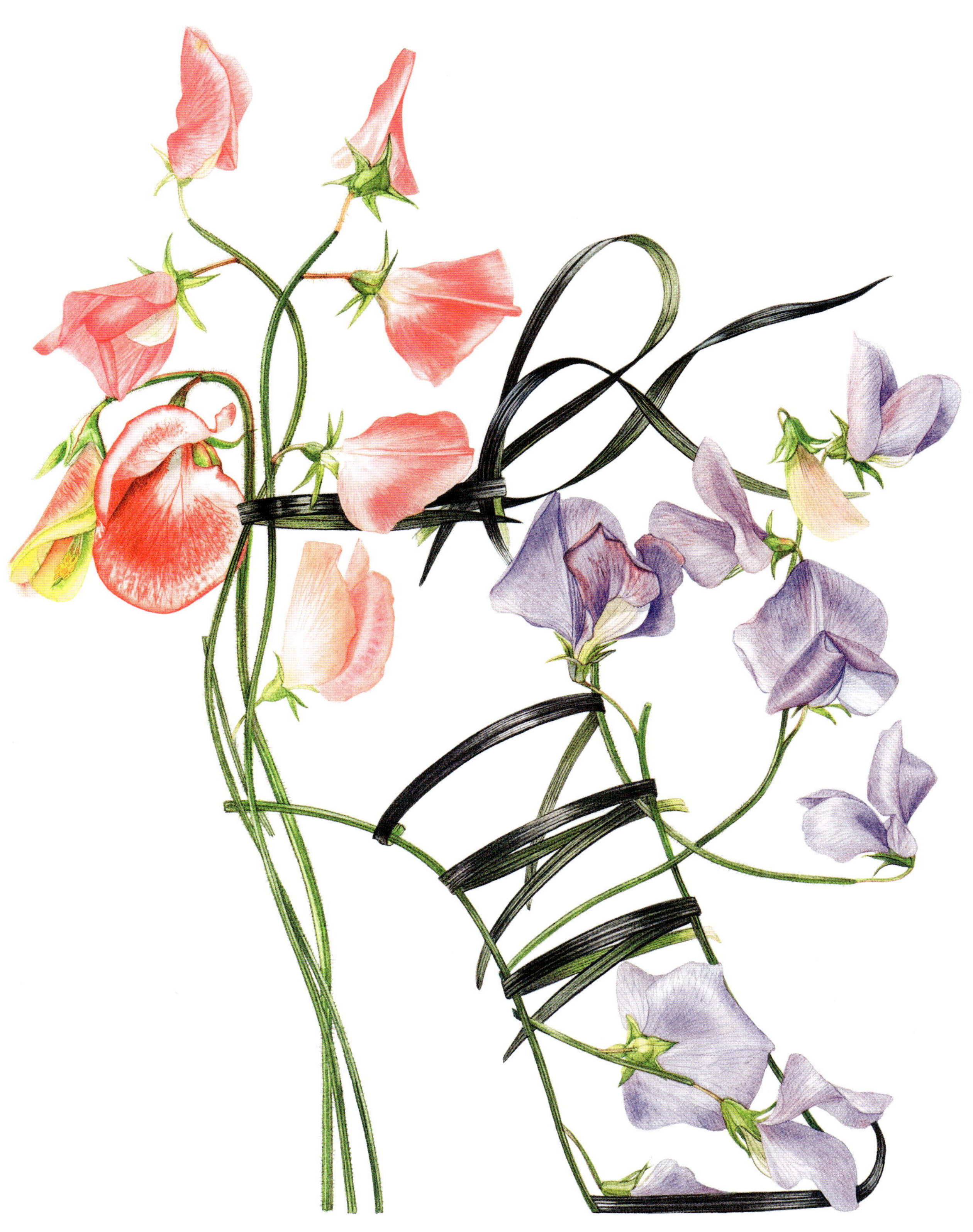

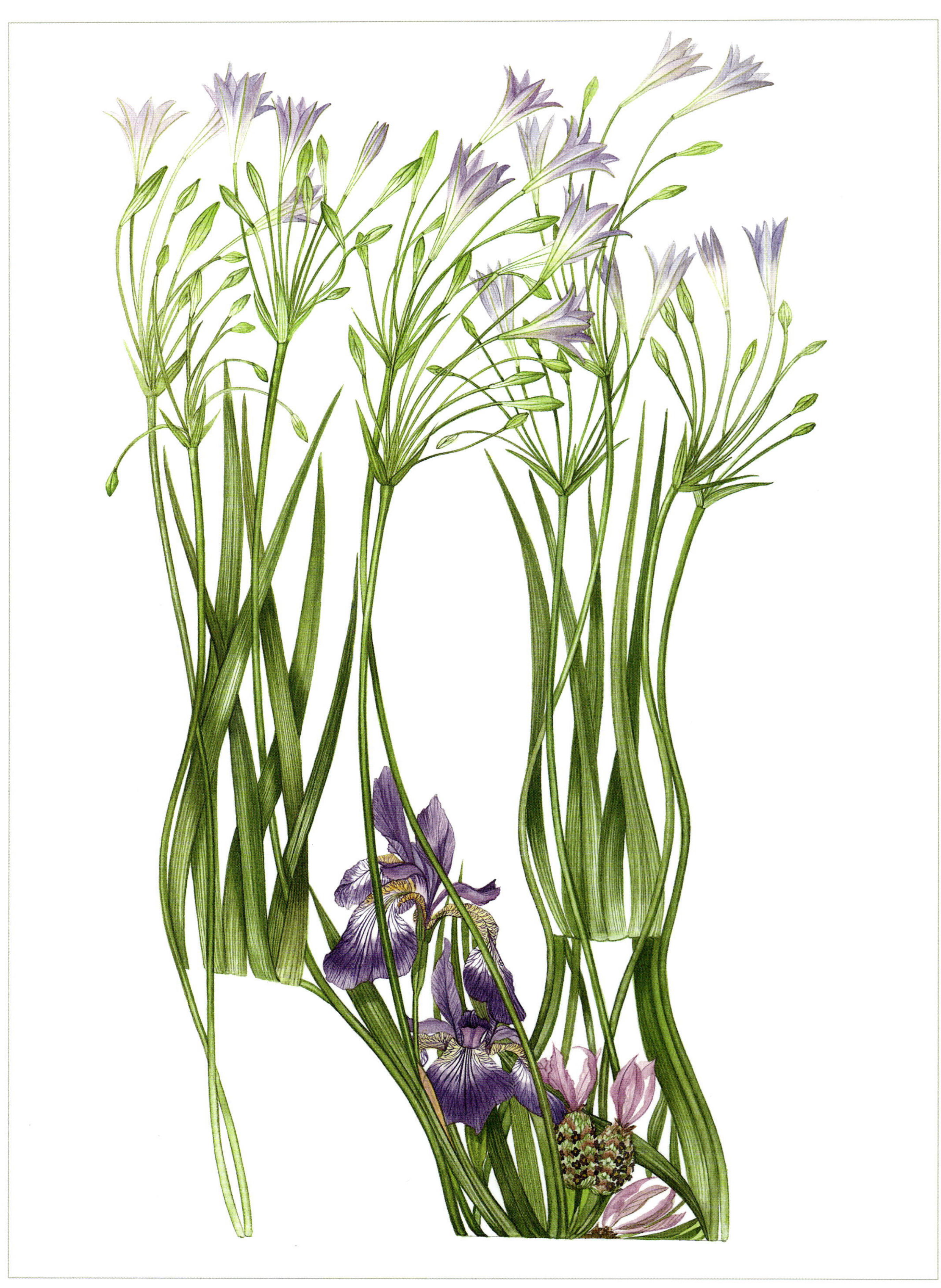

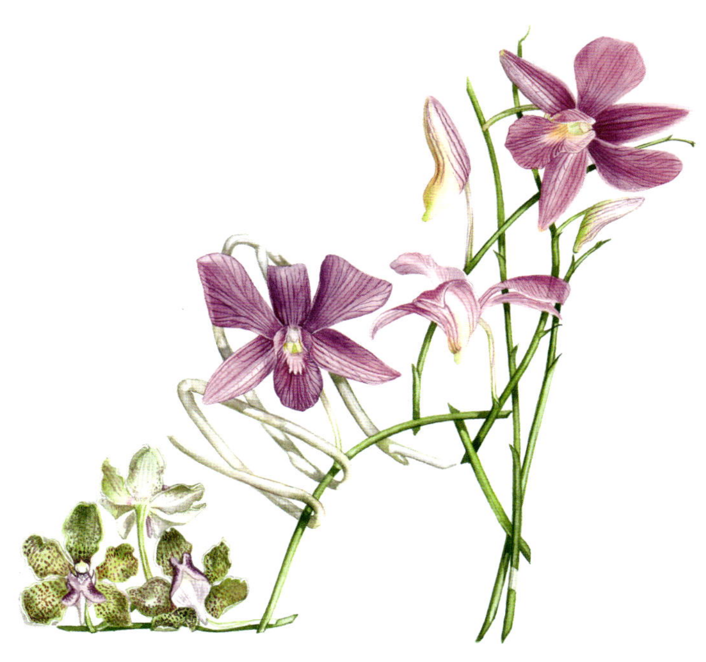

The hot house is sanctuary
Quiet in the heat,
The flowers around us
Fall soaked to our feet.
I lay in heady scent
Succulent, sweet.

And when I sleep
I will dream silent and true,
Of overhanging orchids
And being here with you.

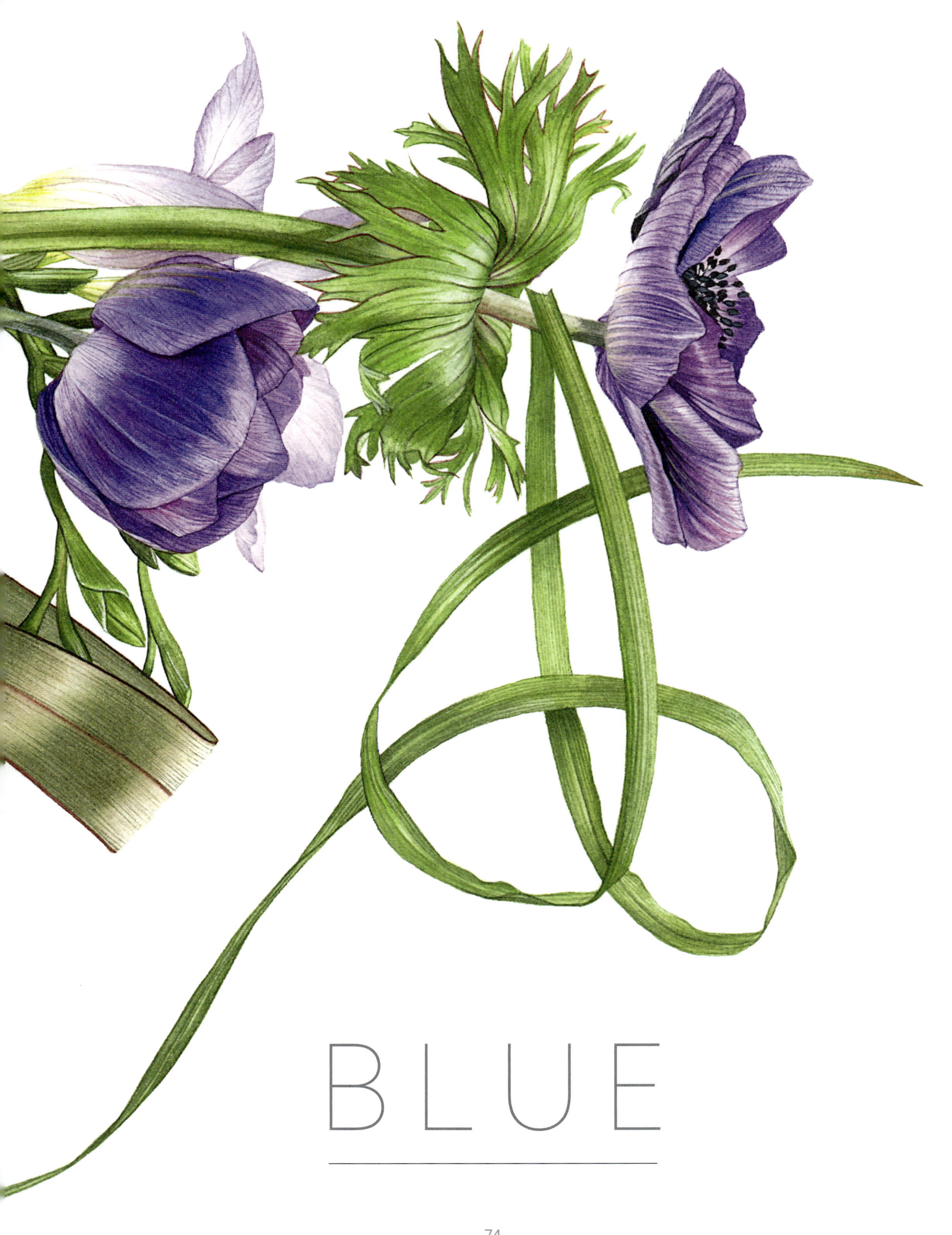
BLUE

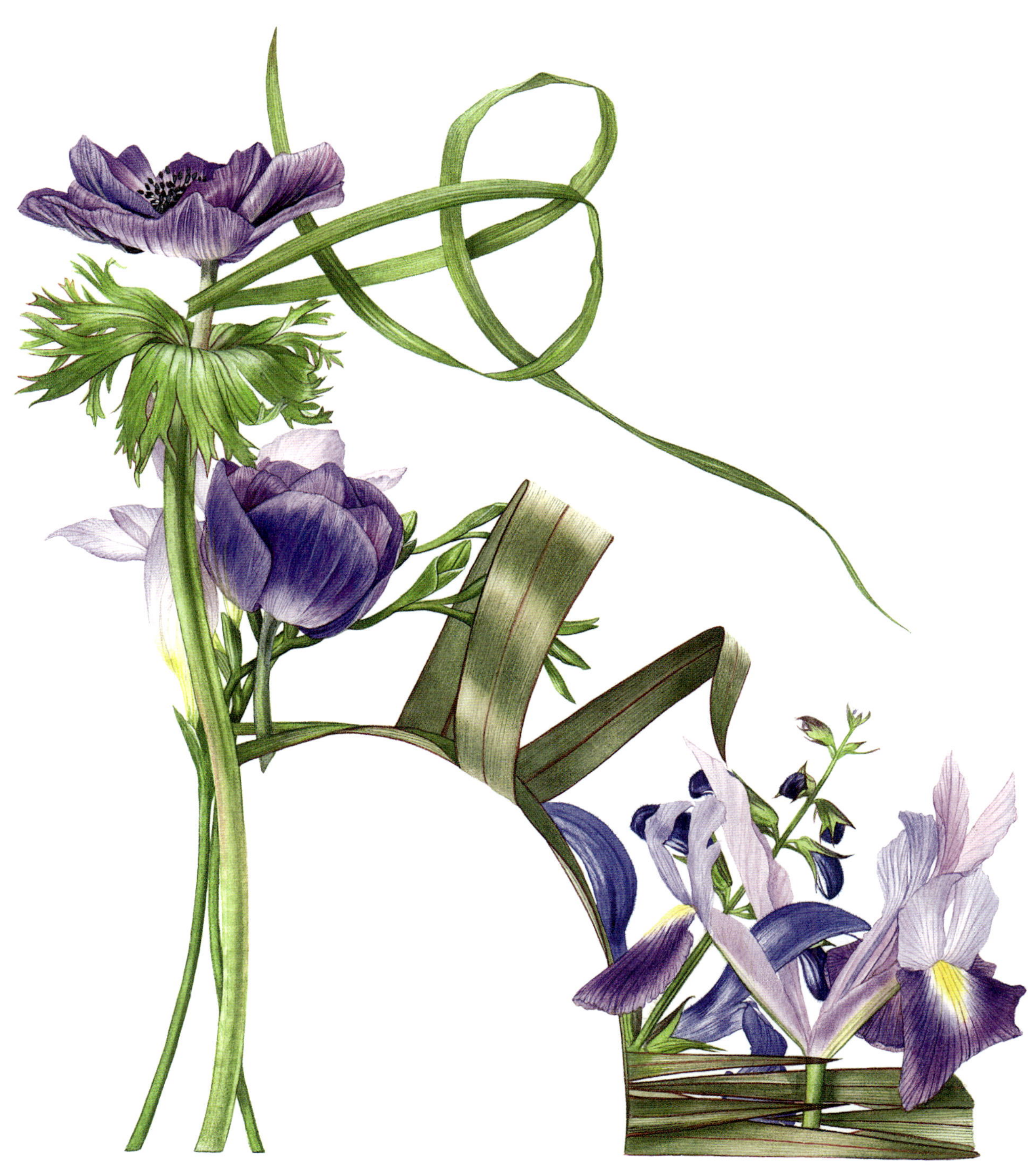

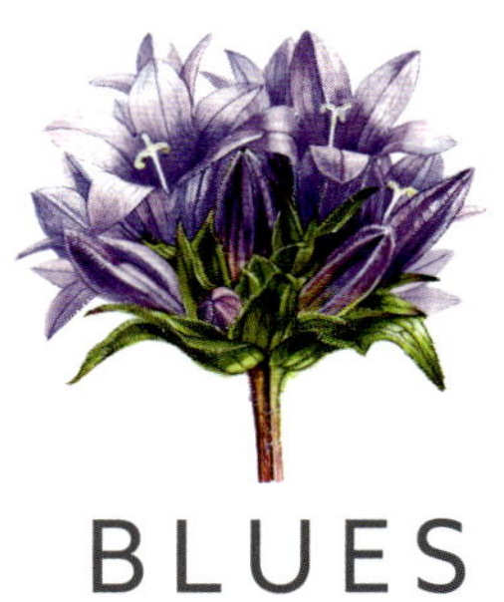

BLUES

S.=Sennelier

COLUMN ONE	COLUMN TWO
S. Phthalocyanine blue + S. Cobalt blue	S. Cobalt blue + S. Rose madder
S. Cobalt blue + S. Lemon	S. French ultramarine + S. Rose madder
S. French ultramarine + S. Lemon	S. Cobalt blue + S. Helios purple
S. Cobalt blue + S. Yellow deep	S. French ultramarine + S. Helios purple
S. French ultramarine + S. Yellow deep	S. French ultramarine + S. Dioxazine purple
S. French ultramarine + S. Phthalocyanine blue	S. French ultramarine + S. Dioxazine purple + S. Cobalt blue
S. French ultramarine + S. Phthalocyanine blue + S. Yellow deep	S. French ultramarine + S. Rose madder
S. Indigo + S. French ultramarine + S. Yellow deep	S. French ultramarine + S. Rose madder + S. Indigo
S. Indigo + S. French ultramarine + S. Quinacridone gold	S. Indigo + S. French ultramarine + S. Dioxazine purple

Soul blue

Lost in blue

London blue

Milk lake

Harbour calm

Mermaid blue

City pearl

Evening drift

Deep lagoon

Dream blue

Blue lapping

Rapture blue

Dolphin dream

Blue opulence

Robe blue

Rich slumber blue

Blue velvet

Blue lavish

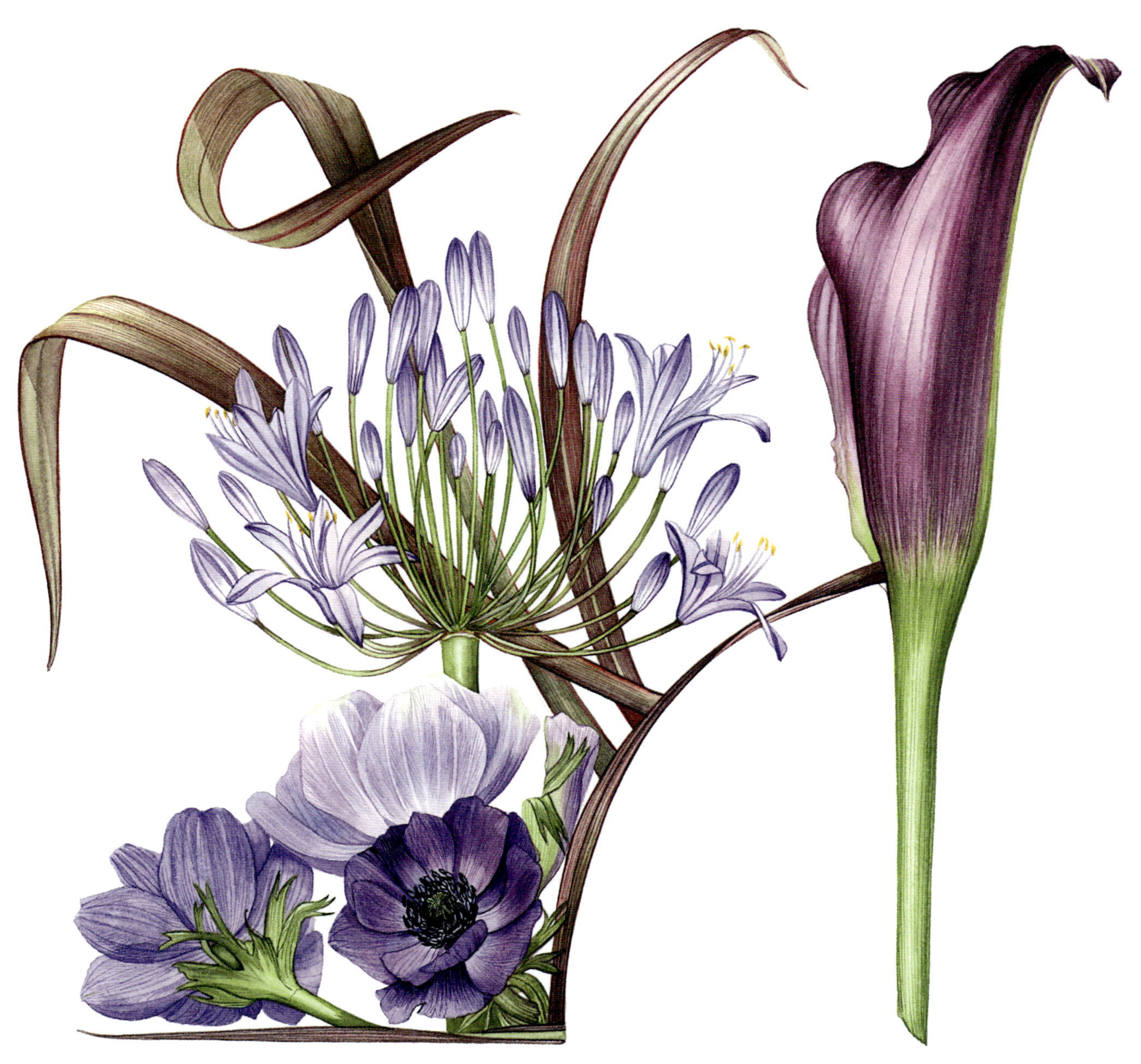

Sometimes a little mystery is more comforting than knowing all the answers.

By Midnight all were looking to the skies
It was from there they would arrive.

All the stars are old as time
some have gone before their shine,
our sweet time's taken making line
and sweep of brush that's so divine.
The stars watch on as we refine
Lines laying in our heart's design.
They will not last, they will decline
But lift us while we ponder time.

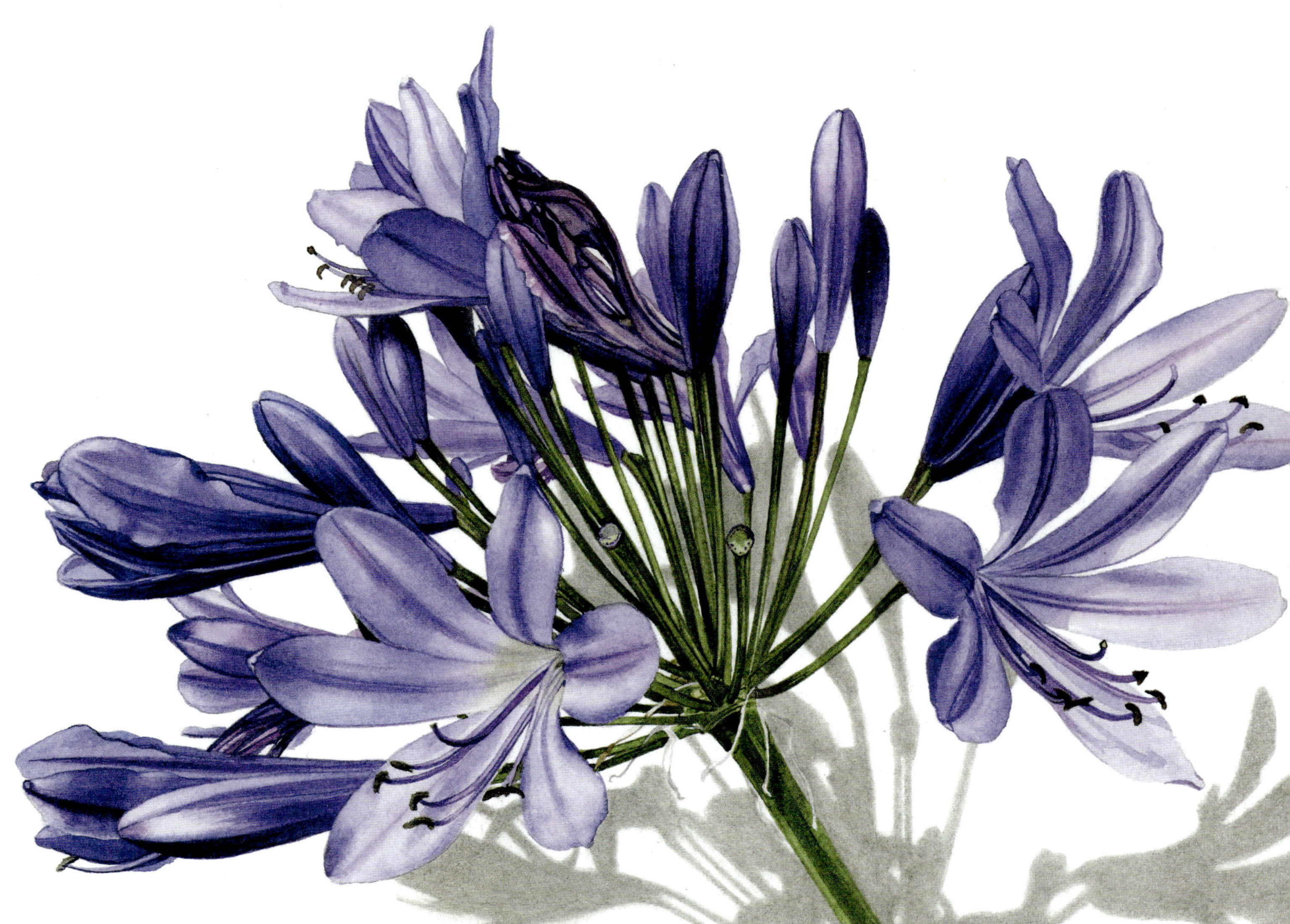

PURPLE
BLACK

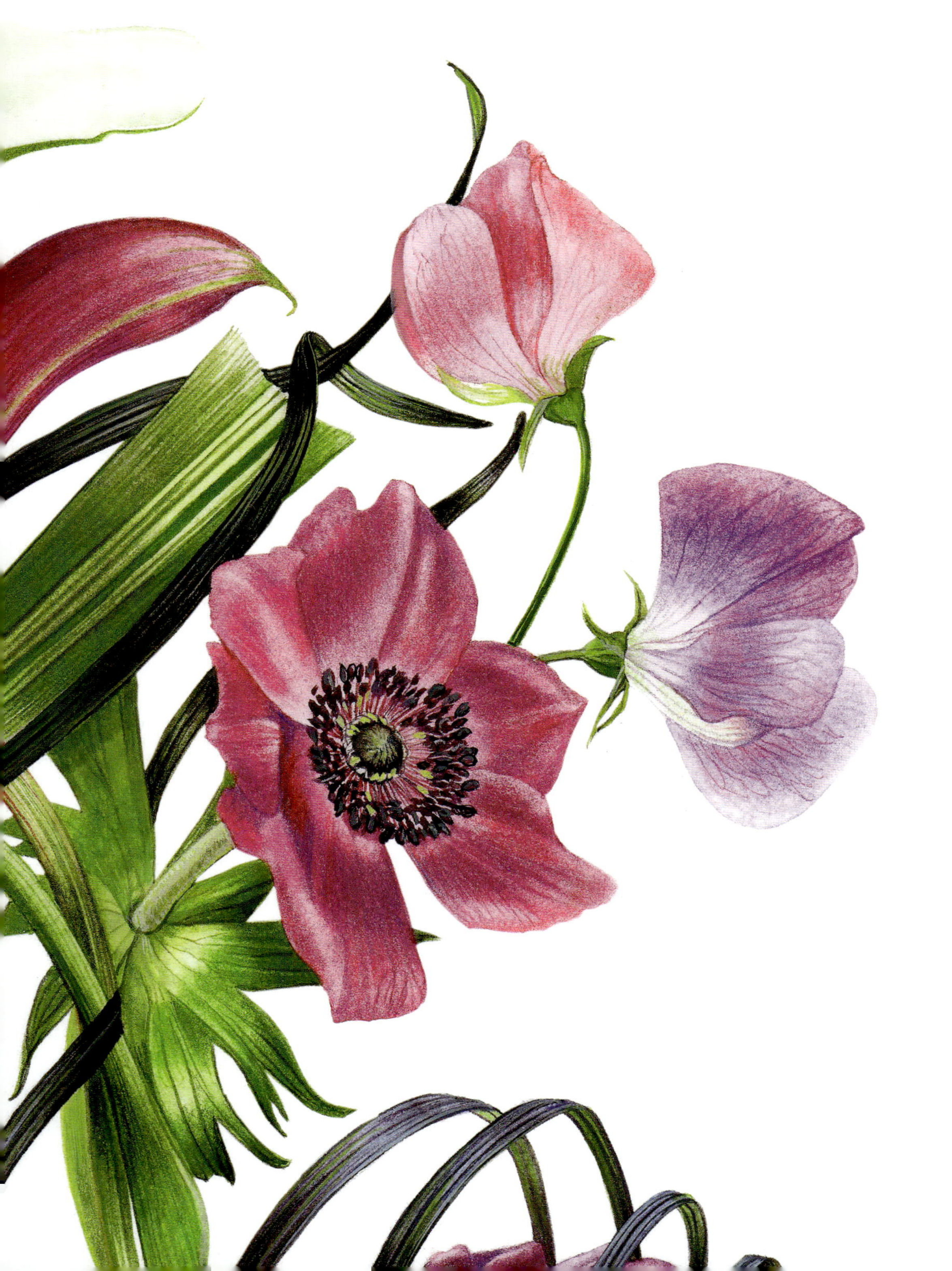

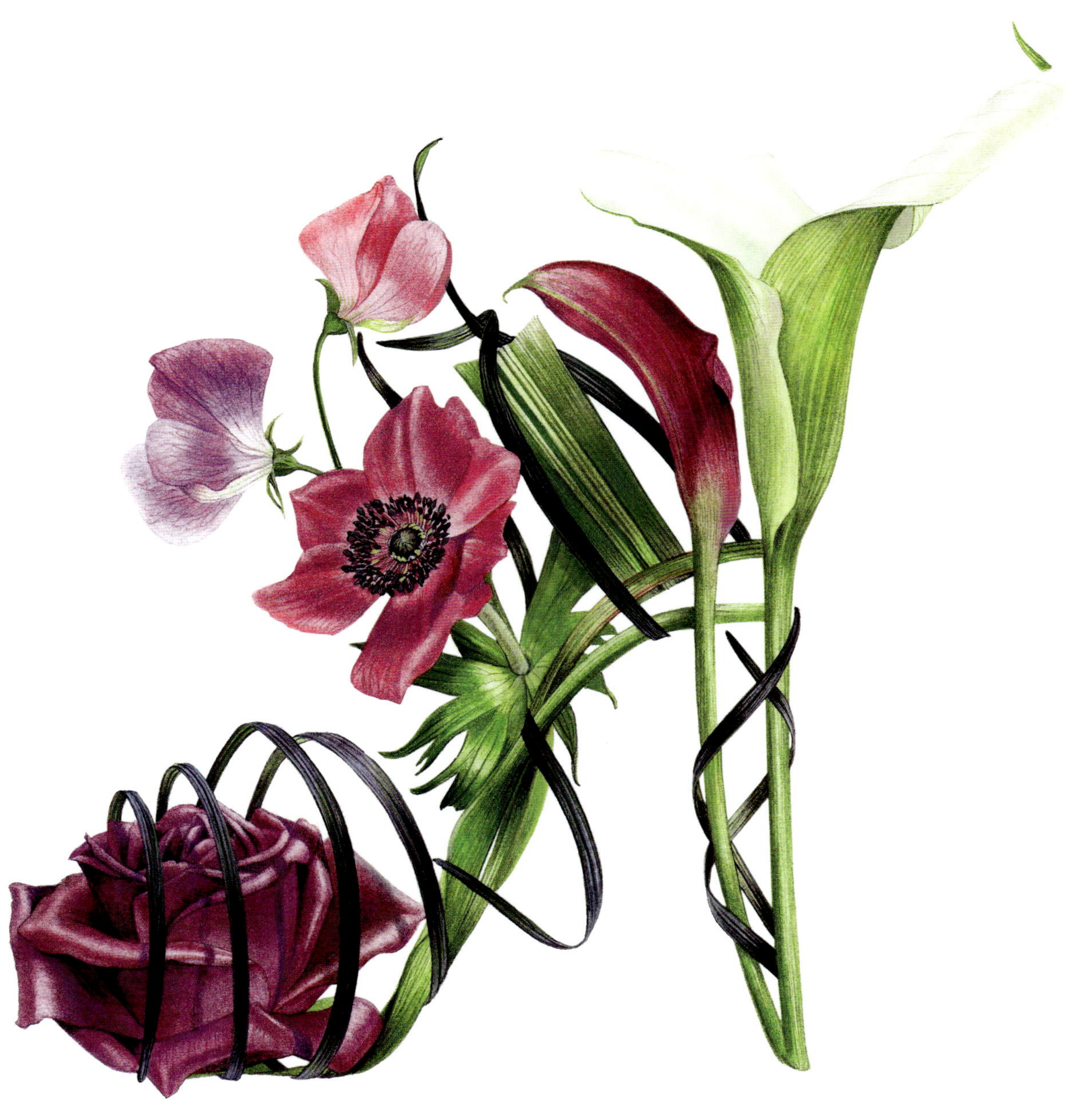

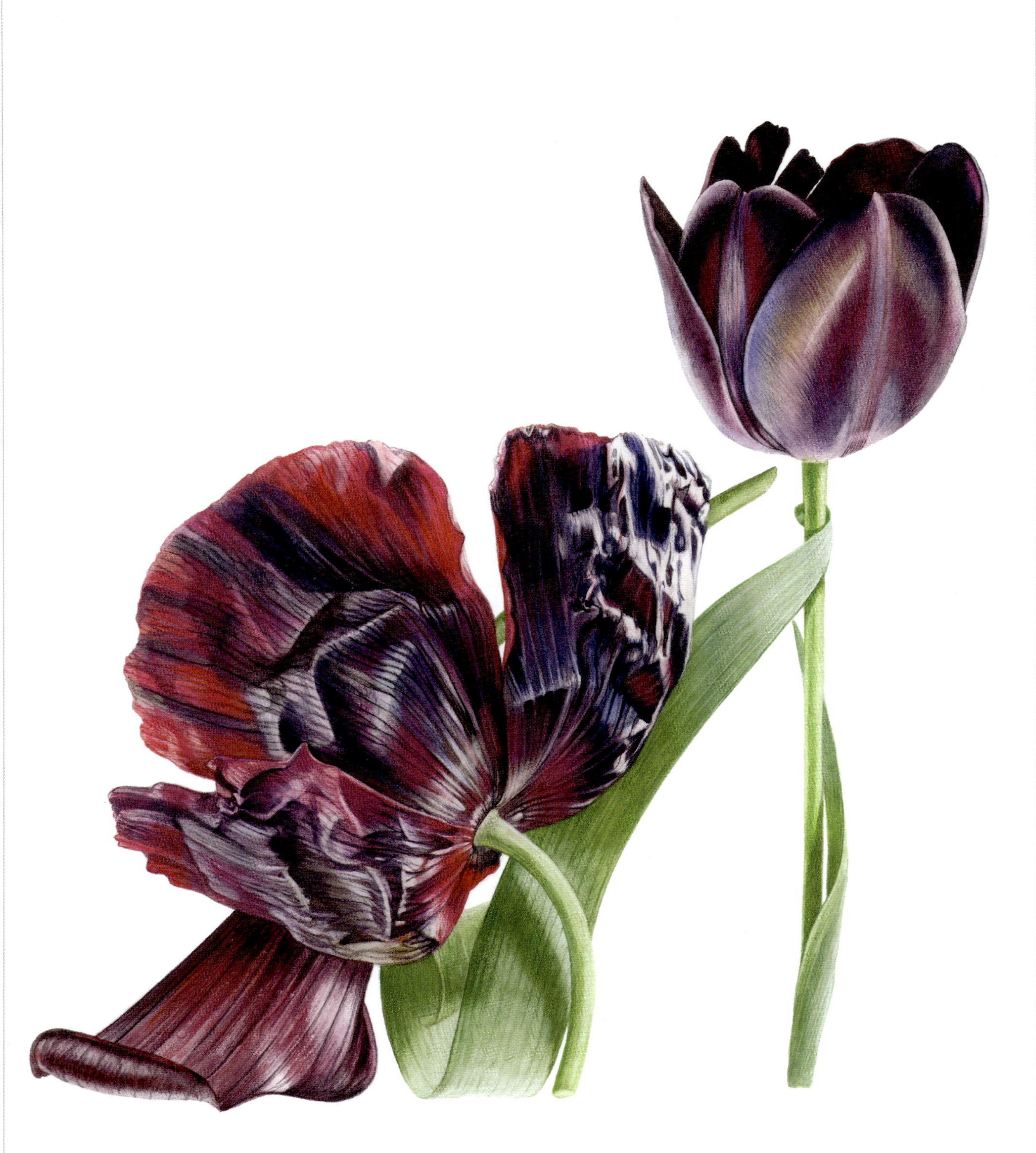

Can you fashion me a pair of shoes that I may be in step with nature?

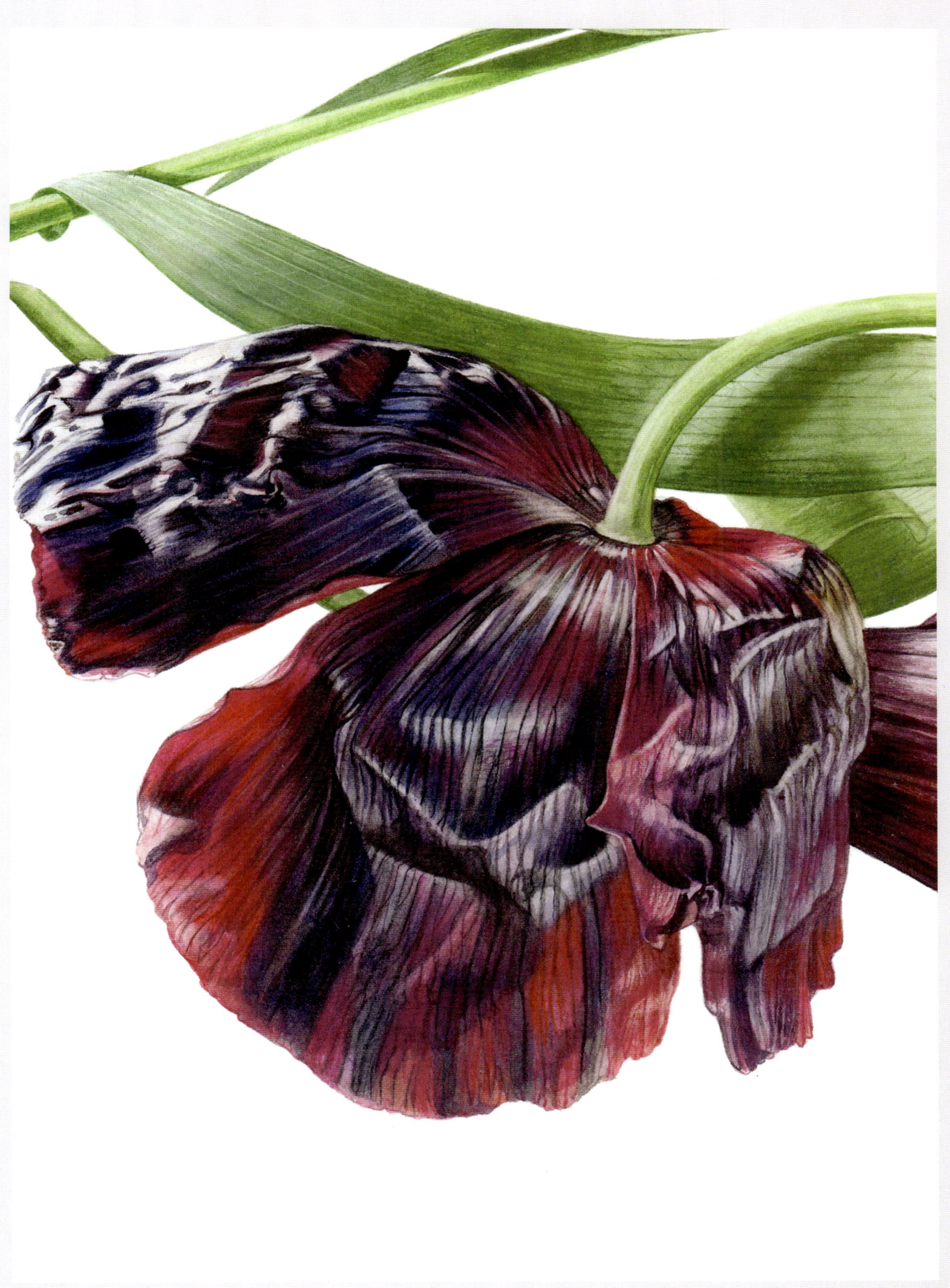

The dark and deep colours are the finest to mix. Some are fulsome and staining, and some are easy to lift.

Take your time to experiment to see which colours stay rich and true when layered and see which lie and dry dull. I love that all the dark blooms have such a rich history and mythology, yet shine out with opulence.

I love that they inspire mystery. Like the night, not all is seen immediately; you must adjust your vision and see the subtle reflection of light in order for the shapes to make sense.

Go as dark as you dare, preserve the light for as long as you can, and paint richly before layering up with dry brushing. Experiment, and don't be afraid of the dark!

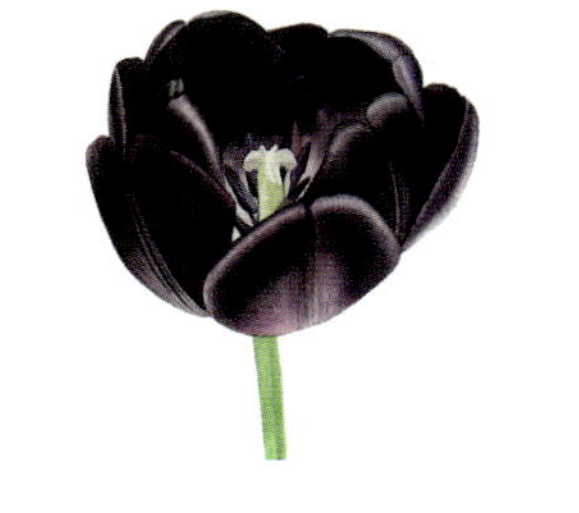

PURPLE BLACKS

S.=Sennelier

COLUMN ONE

S. Blue violet

S. Blue violet + S. Helios purple

S. Helios purple + S. Cobalt blue

S. French ultramarine + S. Rose madder

S. Dioxazine purple + S. Rose madder

S. Quinacridone red + S. Dioxazine purple + S. Rose madder

S. French ultramarine + S. Helios purple

S. French ultramarine + S. Quinacridone red + S. Red

S. French ultramarine + S. Helios purple + S. Quinacridone gold

COLUMN TWO

S. Indigo + S. Yellow deep + S. Rose madder

S. Indigo + S. Red

S. Indigo + S. Red + S. Yellow deep

S. French ultramarine + S. Red + S. Yellow deep

S. Dioxazine purple + S. Yellow deep + S. French ultramarine

S. French ultramarine + S. Phthalocyanine blue + S. Red

S. Dioxazine purple + S. Red + S. Phthalocyanine blue

S. Quinacridone gold + S. French ultramarine + S. Red

S. Indigo + S. Quinacridone gold + S. Red

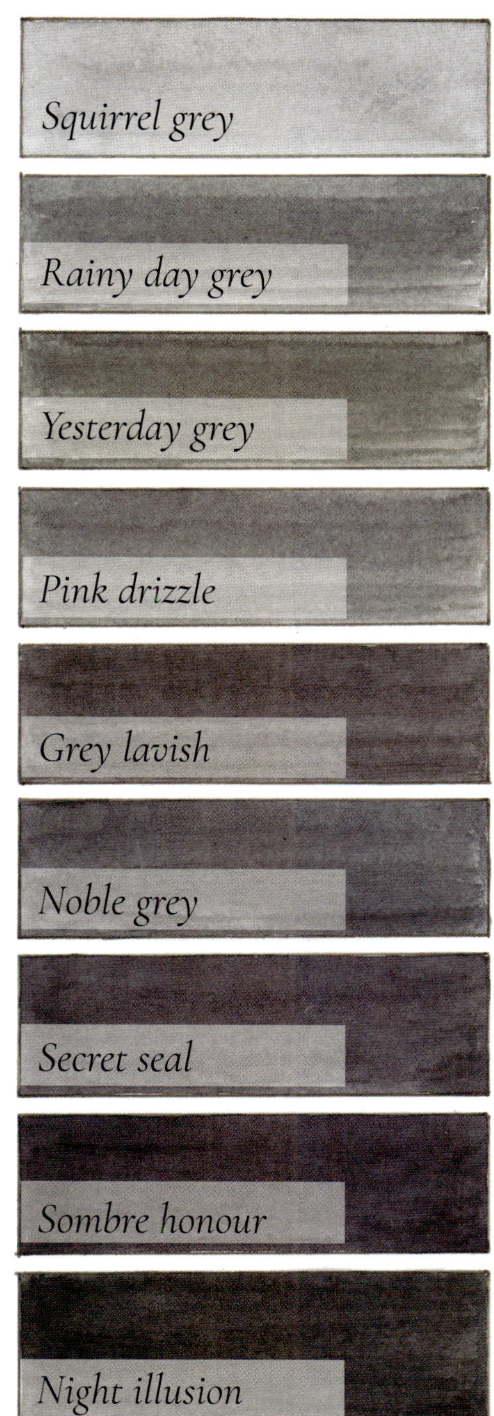

White lake
Lavender haze
Purple rapture
Pale veil
Devotion
Celestial slumber
Royal slipper
Amethyst sleep
Perfect plum
Squirrel grey
Rainy day grey
Yesterday grey
Pink drizzle
Grey lavish
Noble grey
Secret seal
Sombre honour
Night illusion

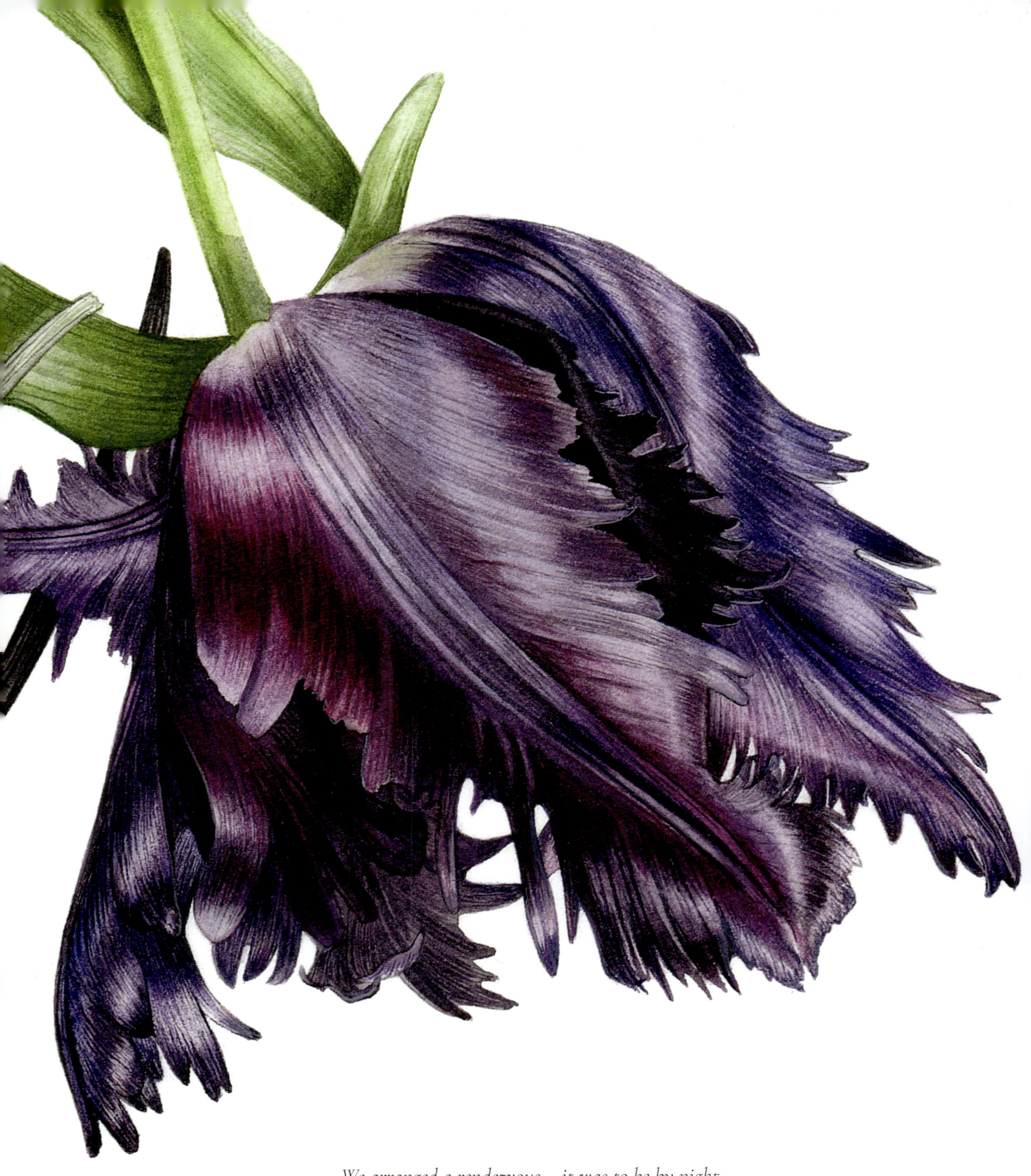

We arranged a rendezvous – it was to be by night.
We stepped in with eyes wide open and kissed with eyes shut tight.
Step softly on my heart, for it is easily broken,
like the petals of a rose, love must be soft and open.

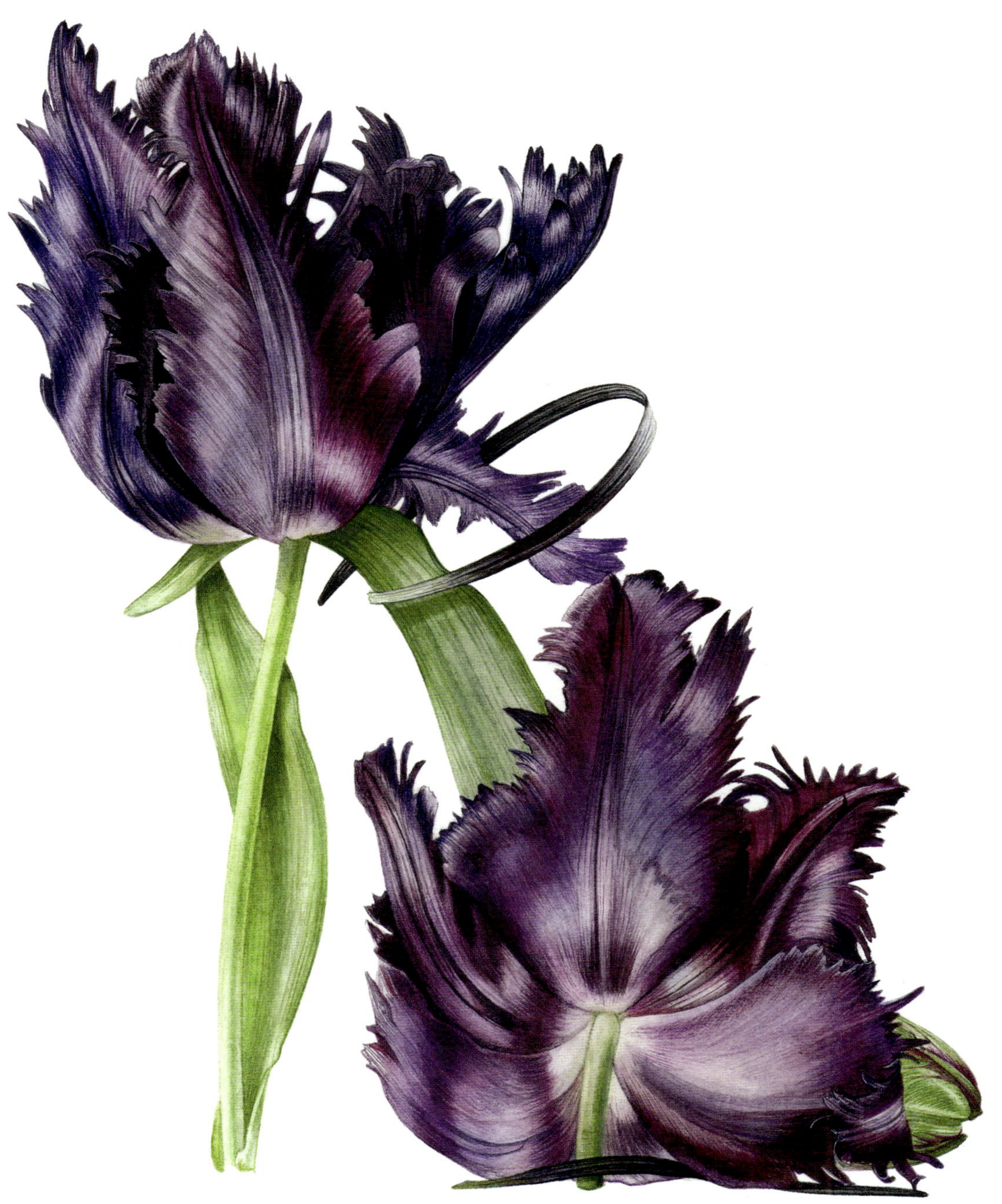

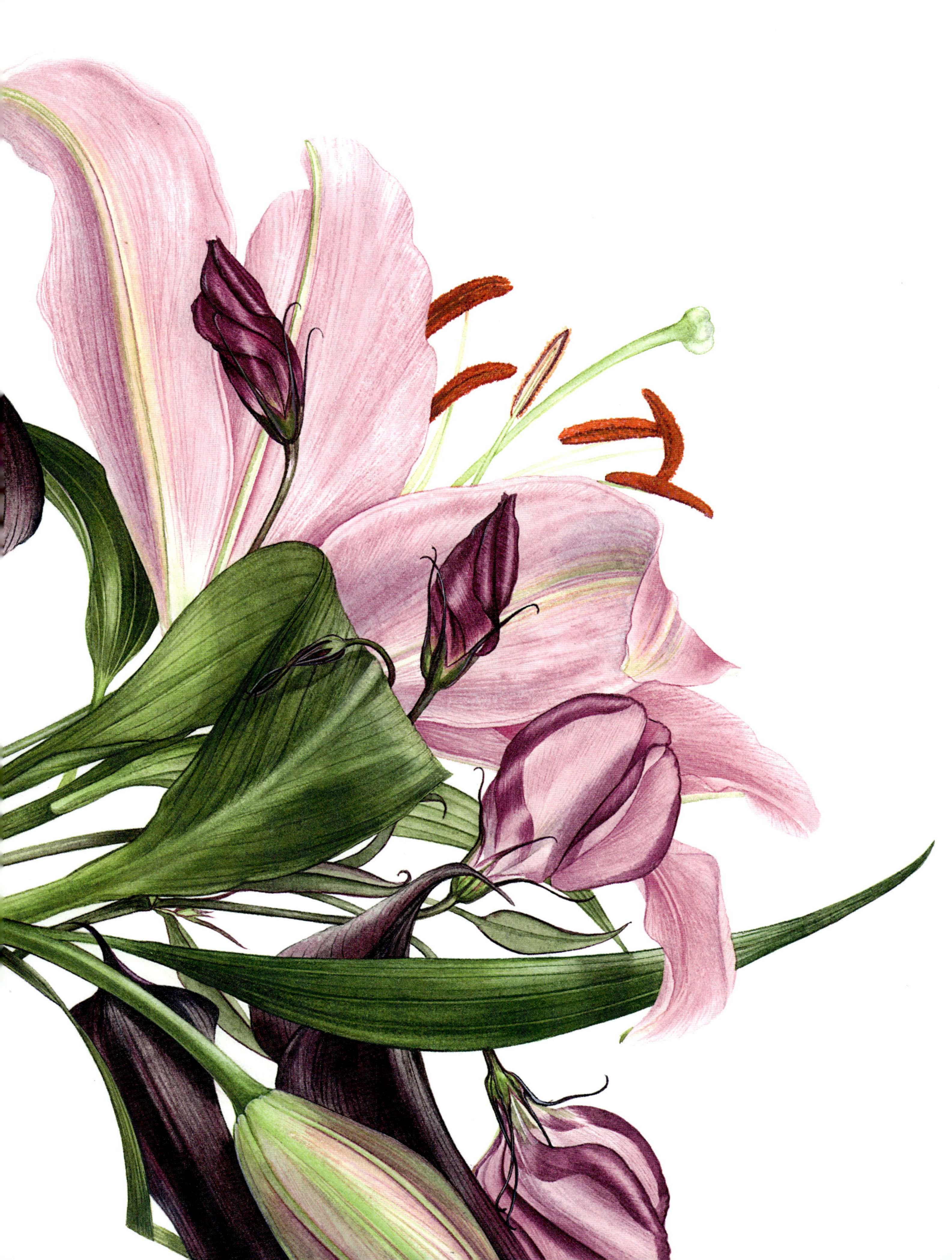

DESTINY

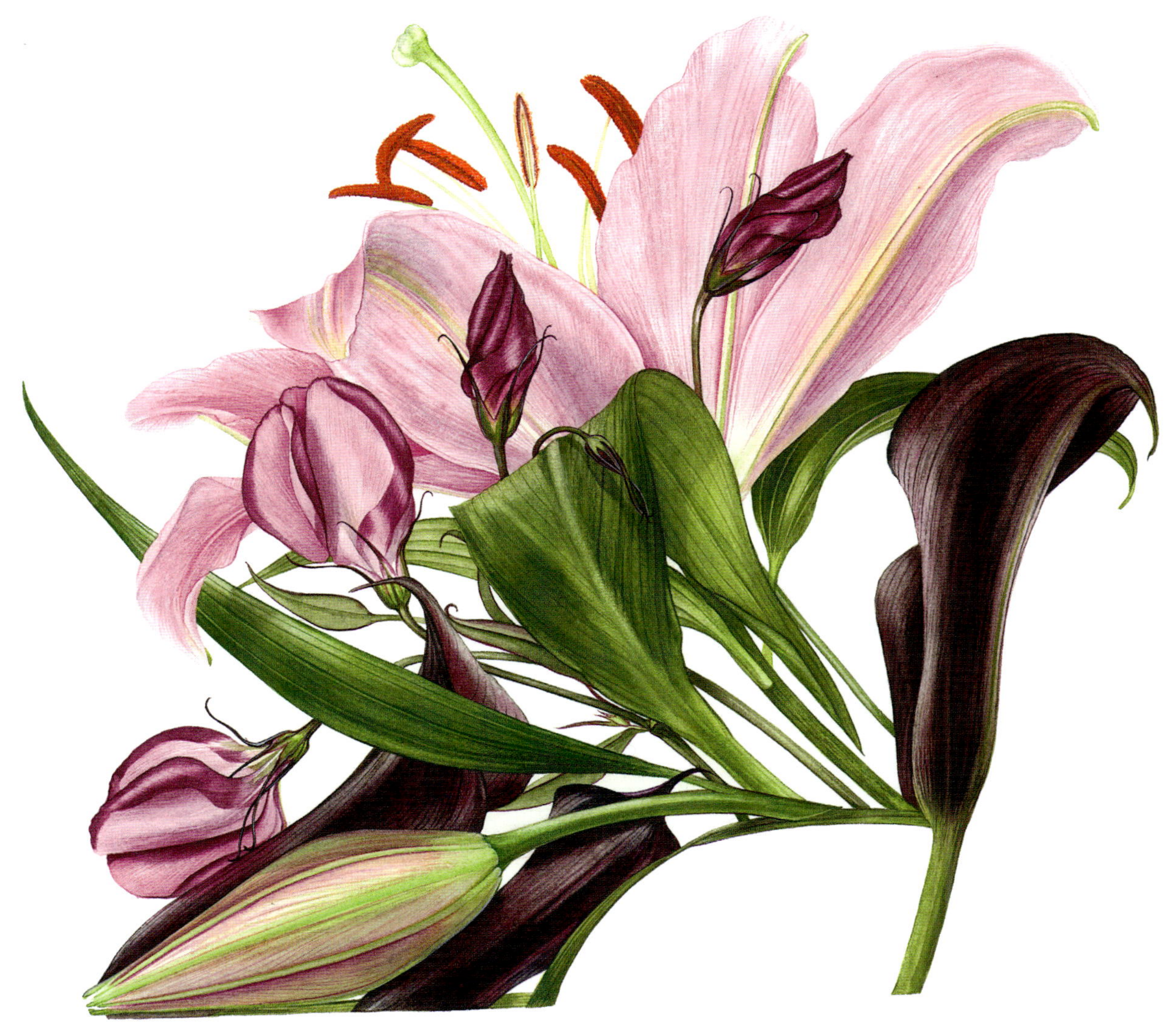

And when the dawn began to break, our destiny appeared;
We had been inside the garden all along.
We had travelled many patterns like all adventurers do,
And found that where we're happiest is the place where we belong.

Put down your tools, let the hammer sleep.
Plant seeds of hope to set strong,
You will find the change in pace surreal,
But you know this is where you belong.

Here we have no need of shoes,
the earth is soft, forgiving,
We leave the soil to rest undisturbed,
to embrace new ways of living.

Our hands seek rest,
Our minds to settle and contemplate within.
A desire to bend with nature
as trees to the prevailing wind.

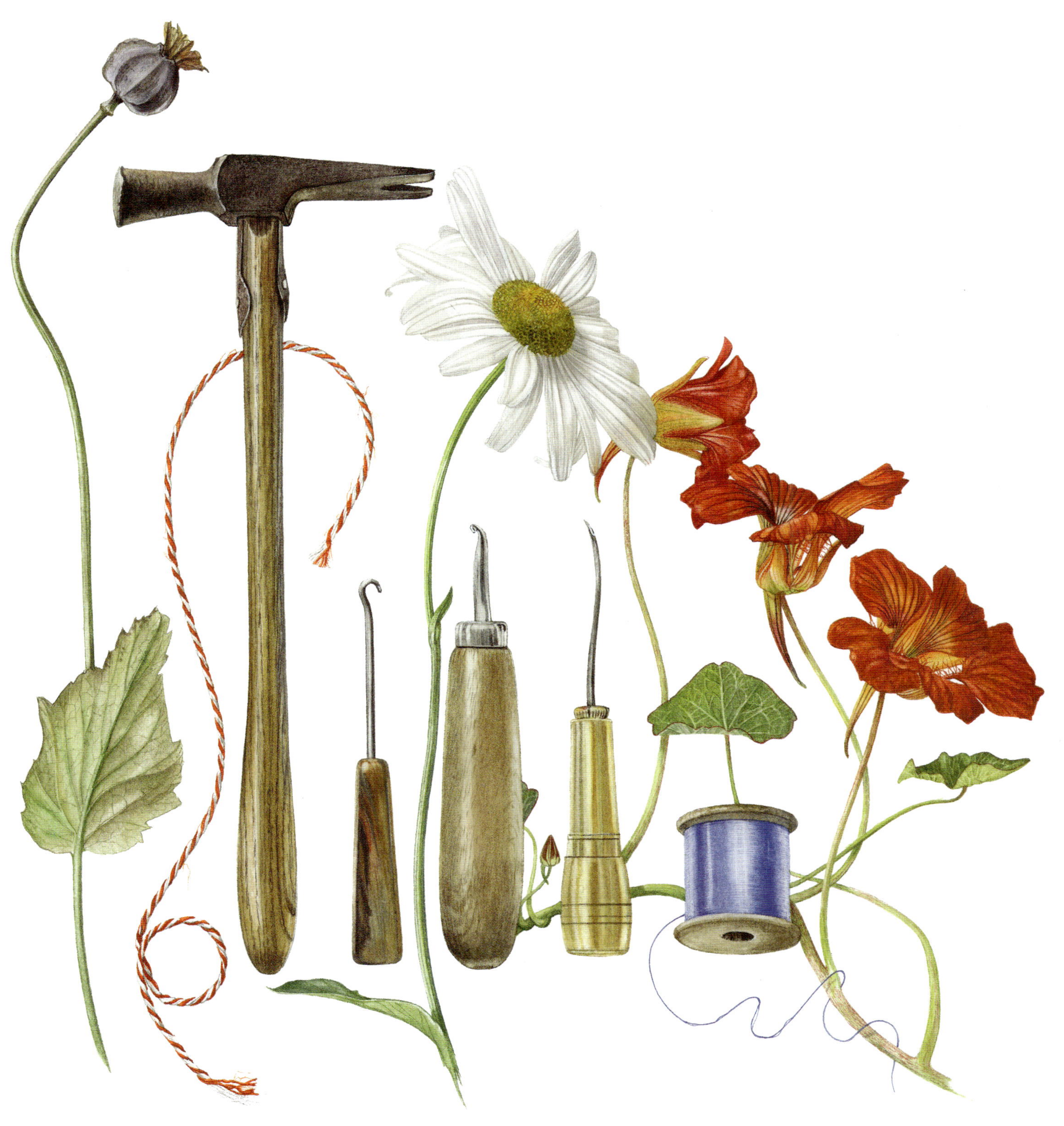

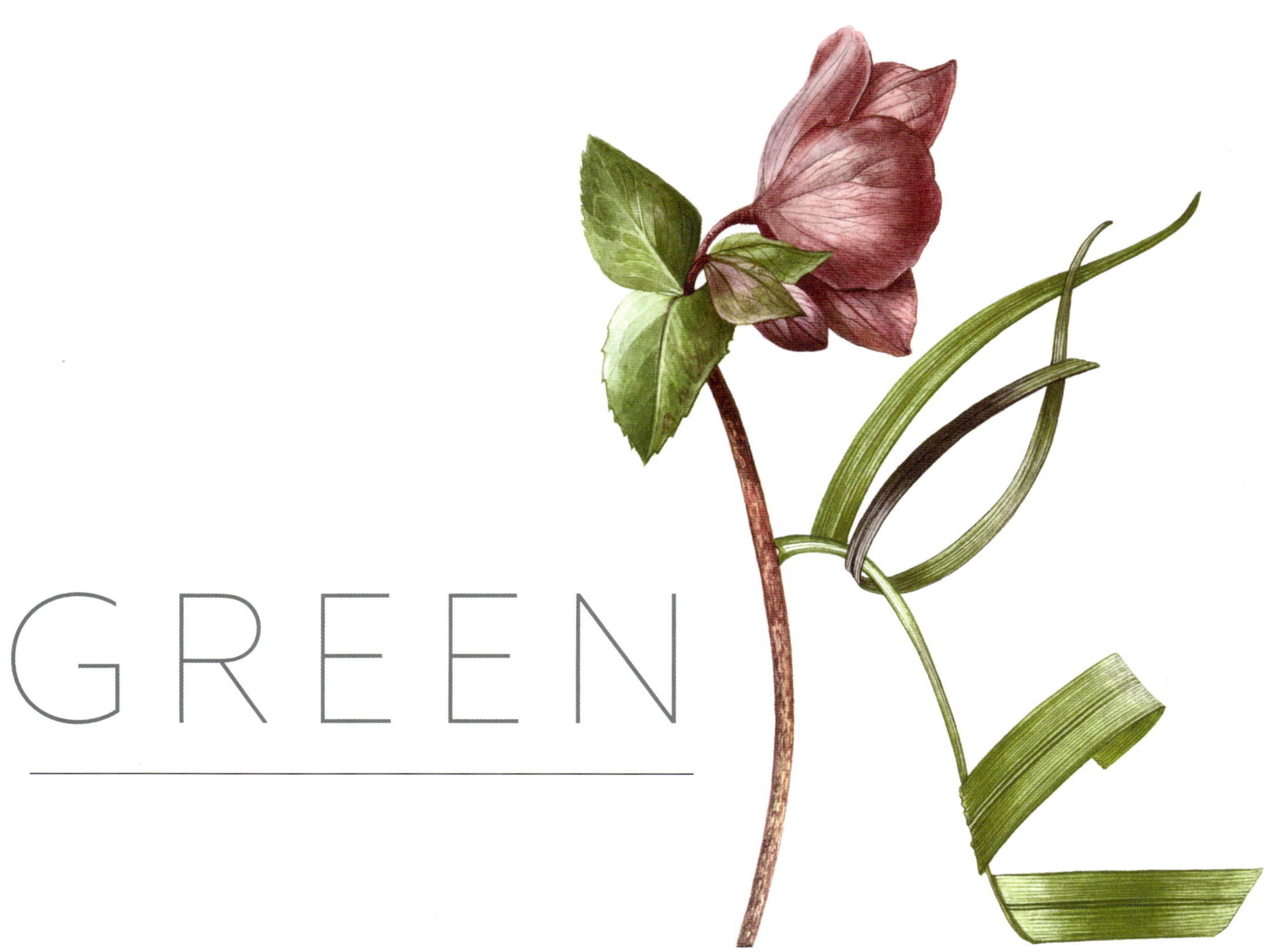

GREEN

GREENS

S.=Sennelier

COLUMN ONE

S. Lemon + S. Phthalocyanine blue

S. Lemon + S. Cobalt blue

S. Lemon + S. French ultramarine

S. Lemon + S. Yellow deep + S. French ultramarine

S. Quinacridone gold + S. Phthalocyanine blue

S. Quinacridone gold + S. Phthalocyanine blue + S. Lemon

S. Lemon + S. French ultramarine

S. Yellow deep + S. Phthalocyanine blue + S. Lemon

S. Yellow deep + S. Phthalo Blue + S. Lemon + French ultramarine

COLUMN TWO

S. Quinacridone gold + S. Phthalocyanine blue

S. Quinacridone gold + S. Phthalocyanine blue + S. Rose madder

S. Quinacridone gold + S. Cobalt blue

S. Quinacridone gold + S. Cobalt blue + S. Yellow deep

S. French ultramarine + S. Quinacridone gold

S. French ultramarine + S. Quinacridone gold + S. Lemon

S. Quinacridone gold + S. Indigo

S. Quinacridone gold + S. Indigo + S. Red

S. French ultramarine + S. Red + S. Phthalo Blue + S. Quinacridone gold

COLUMN ONE	COLUMN TWO
New life	*Green pool*
Sunshine seeker	*Soft seed*
Cream green	*Haymaker*
Harvest hope	*Wet hay*
Leaf dust	*Dusk promise*
Young spring	*Evening meadow*
Song thrush green	*Secret shade*
My green place	*Late summer night*
Woodland dawn	*Woodland eve*

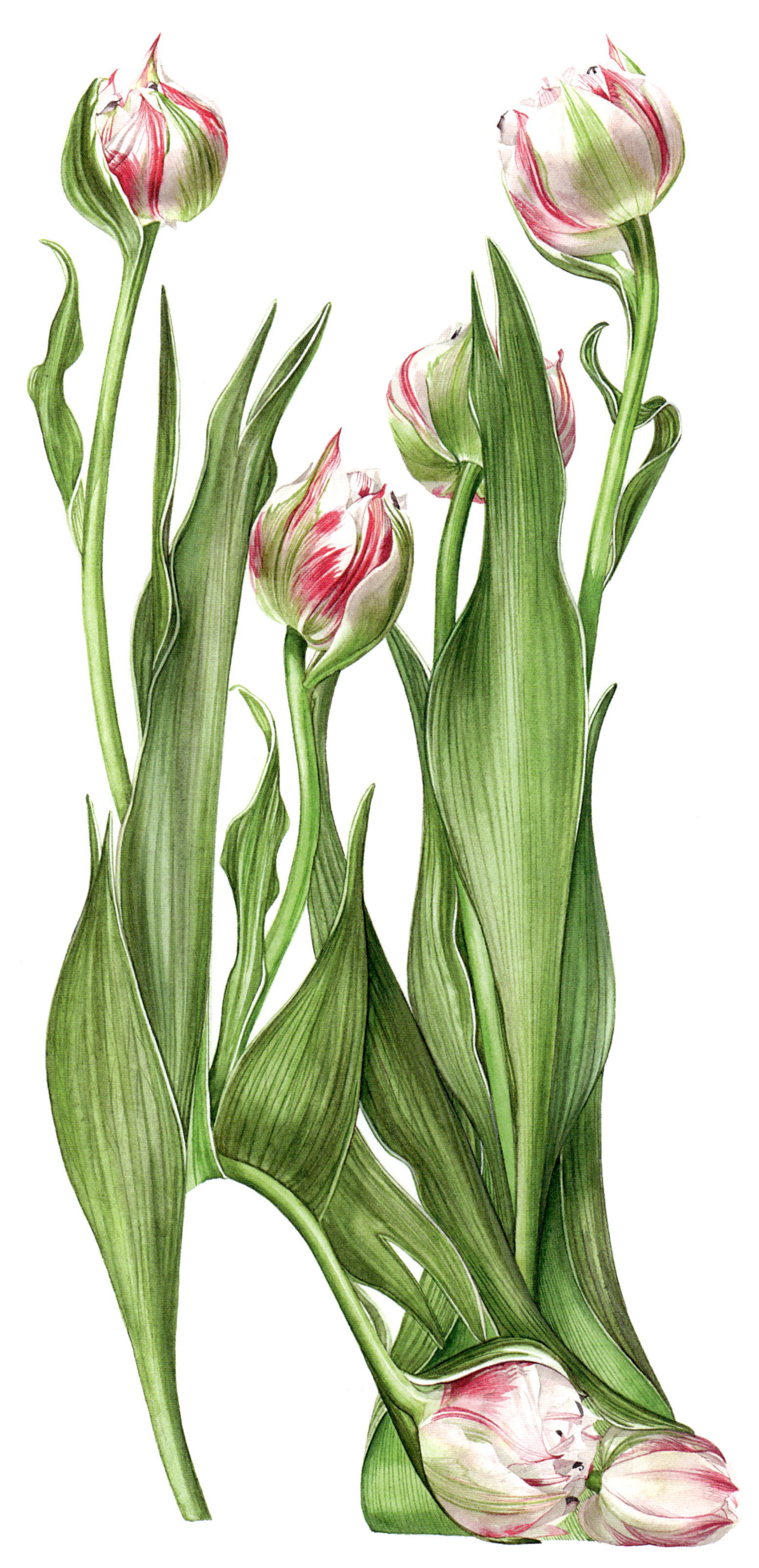

Can we become the gardeners?
Calm and kind in tune.
Nurture plants in verdant soil,
Anointed in the dew.

Green is where my heart is. It is the best colour of them all. You may know that, as humans, our hunter-gatherer ancestry has left us with the ability to see the subtlest differences in the colour green. Our eyes have developed to perceive more green shades than any other colour. It could be the smallest depression in a field of grasses, seemingly all the same colour, and yet we see a path.

Greens are a delight to mix, and I have always chosen to mix mine from blues and yellows and experiment with adding other colours to attain the perfect green. I am not a fan of fixed colour theory, instead choosing to play and discover colour for myself. I read a quote somewhere and I think it went: *...to always follow the precedence is to forego thinking.*

It reminded me of a chemistry lesson that I had at school, where we were led to a certain point in an experiment and then encouraged to imagine or work out for ourselves what came next.

To be shown that we can decide or make a choice about something that may already have a conclusion, to be told that we could, if we chose to, find our own solution, was enlightening. Perfect teaching, perhaps?

Green is such a soothing colour. It rests our eyes and connects us with all that is verdant. Embrace the colour green.

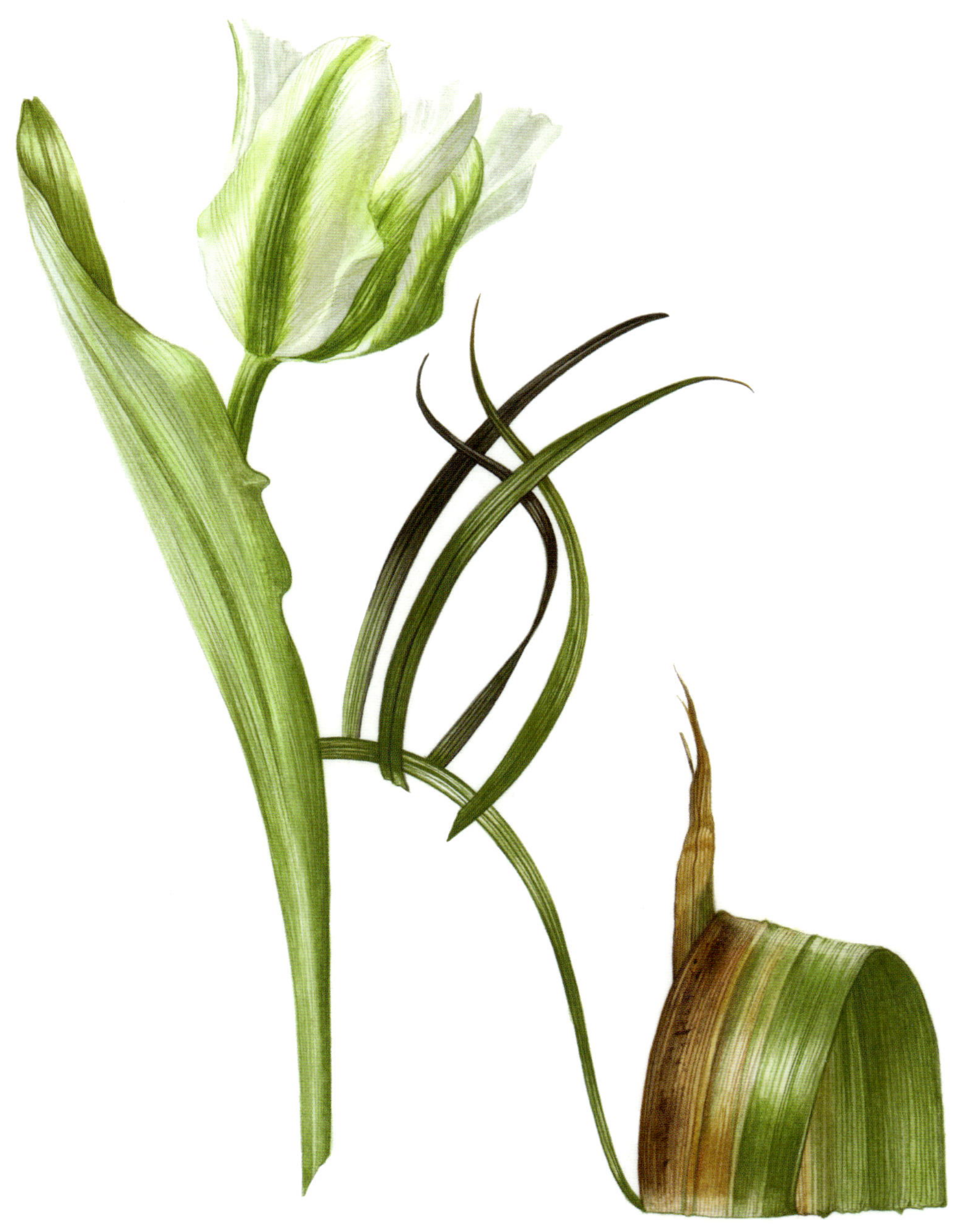

When the light is aureate and the blooms are set to sleep,
We see our love for earth is golden, precious, kind and deep.

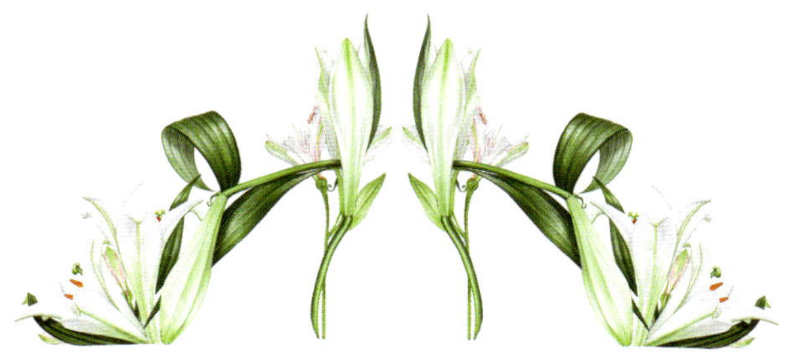

REFLECTION

I hope you have enjoyed the journey through my shoe collection, and the little moments of thought to which they are paired. My shoes are painted to escape the ordinary of every day.

The ideas that accompany them are little snippets of poetry or prose that reflect on a virtual journey, running from the indoors and into the garden of the world outside. I write these little thoughts in my notebooks and have chosen the ideas that seem most appropriate to my shoes. The plants I have selected for each shoe help me recall the places that I have been and seen, and the moments which eventually led me to where I am today.

When I was a child, my family and I moved to live in the countryside. It was a brief spell where we embarked on many adventures. The time we shared, surrounded by woodlands, fields and animals buried itself deep into my heart. Ever since then, I have been hoping for and seeking a return to life in a rural setting. Our small, family adventure, which lasted just three beautiful years, ingrained in me a love of flowers, grasses, scent and season.

In city, town or country, every plant is precious, and for me, each deserves celebration. The seasons change, and the forever busy wildlife get on with their day, and all the plants are constantly finding ways to seek the sun with a hope for tomorrow. My metaphor of searching for a garden came to light as I was continually making and nurturing memories through my paintings of the flowers that have inspired me along the way: a floral journey, if you wish. A garden, however small, may not be ours forever but we can prepare it for the next gardener (or indeed for mother nature to gently re-embrace). Not all seek the countryside, but for those that do, I hope you find it and I hope you treat it well. I think we all drift on the breeze of destiny, seeking a place where our feet will settle and hoping to find that special place to flourish.

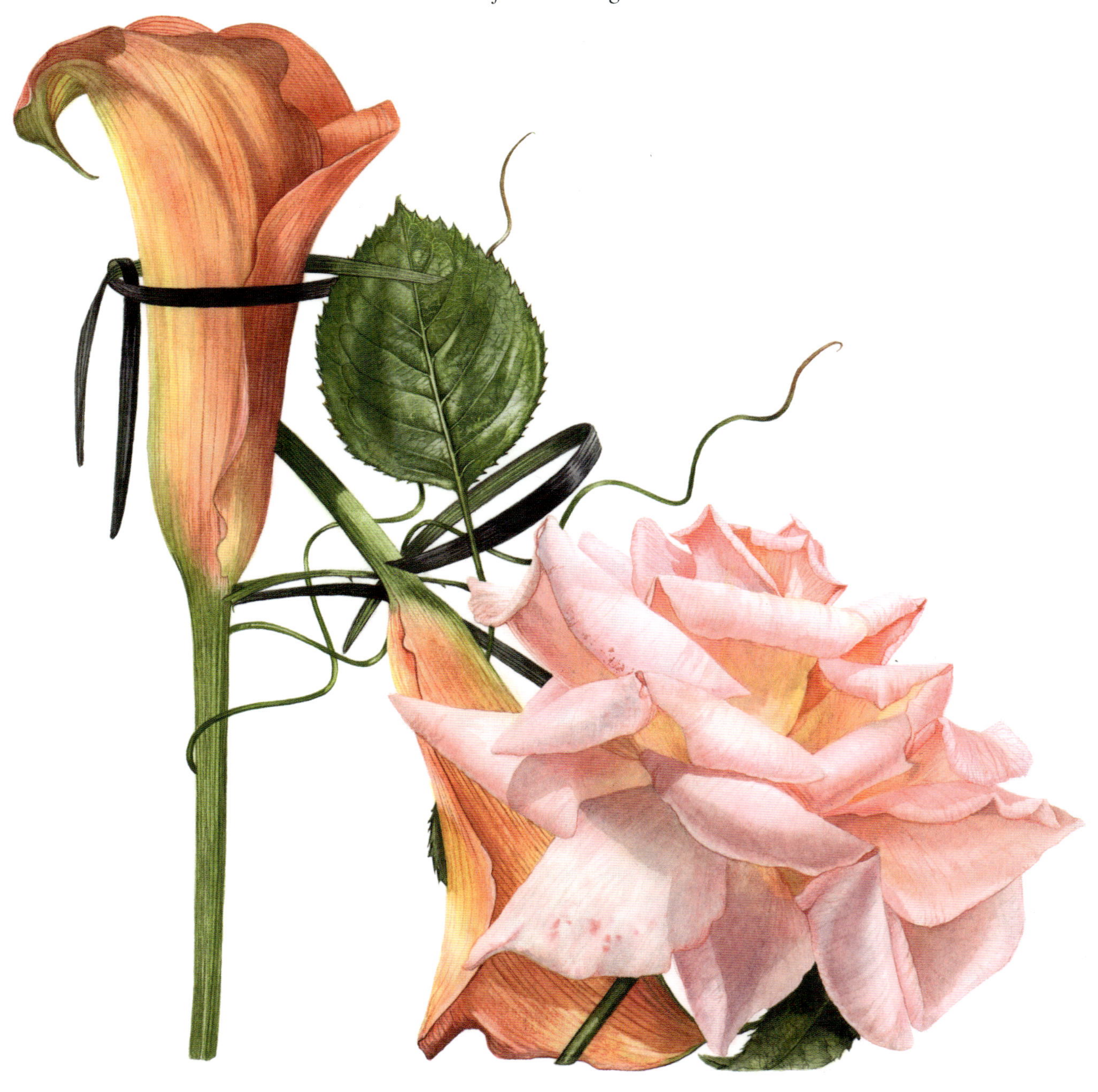

When shadows fall long
And forward moves slow,
We will see our desire path
To sanctuary, to home.
Are we not always seeking?
A place to call home.
A place to find solace,
Where flowers can grow.

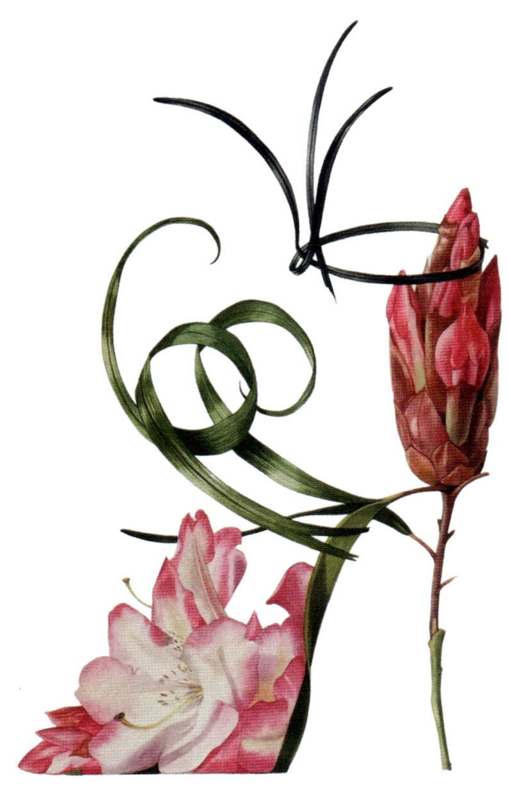

The valley's sweet caressing air,
patterned webs hang with dew and sparkle there.
Grass, the home of many we don't see,
Entwined and woven so beautifully.
They make their life in the softest sway,
Nestled safe to greet each day.

I looked down to see the luscious roots
grow thick beneath my feet;
no need to travel anymore,
as this will be our destiny,
and this will be the canopy
beneath which we will shelter.

THE SHOES, PAINTINGS AND THEIR

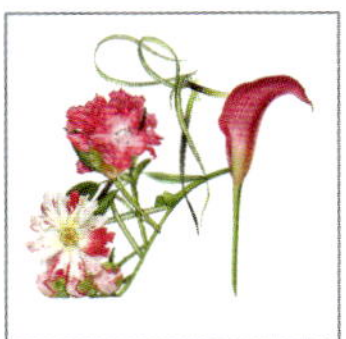

Front cover, title page and **page 17**, 'Frida'
(Rhododendron Rose Shoe)
Rhododendron 'Fantastica',
Zantedeschia aethiopica 'Sumatra',
Paeonia lactiflora 'Sarah Bernhardt',
Rosa 'Crazy for You'

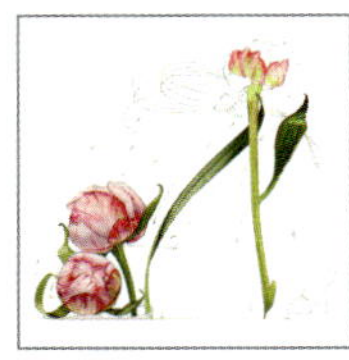

Page 15, 'Anna'
(The Shoemaker's Shoe)
Paeonia lactiflora 'Sarah Bernhardt'

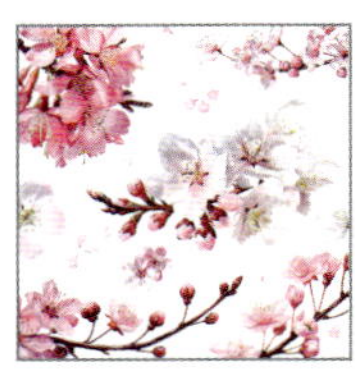

Inside front endpapers, 'Cherry Blossoms, Various'

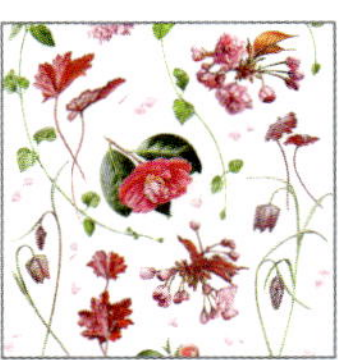

Page 16, 'Spring Pattern'
Heuchera 'Fire Chief'
Camellia japonica 'Dr King'
Prunus 'Royal Burgundy'
Snake's head fritillary – *Fritillaria meleagris*
Greater periwinkle – *Vinca major*

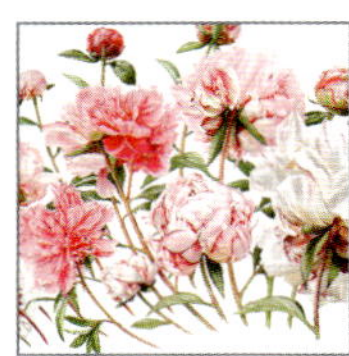

Pages 2 and 3, 'A Passion for Peonies'
Paeonia lactiflora 'Sarah Bernhardt'
Paeonia lactiflora 'Shirley Temple'
Paeonia lactiflora 'Kansas'

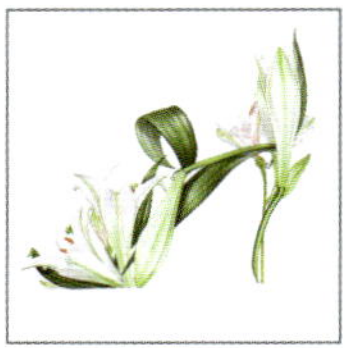

Pages 22 and 97, 'Sophie'
(White Shoe)
Lily – *Lilium longiflorum*
Alstroemeria 'Duke François'

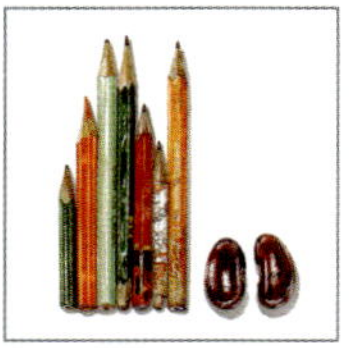

Page 4, 'Alongside'
(Pencils and runner bean seeds)
Runner bean seeds – *Phaseolus coccineus*

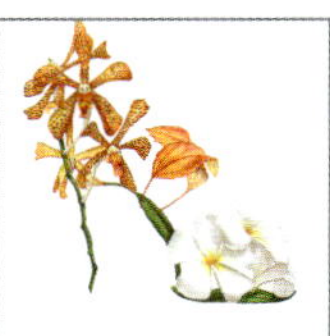

Page 23, 'Abraha'
(Orange Orchid Shoe)
Yellow spotted spider orchid – *Orchidaceae*
Frangipani – *Plumeria sp.*
Japanese persimmon – *Diospyros kaki*

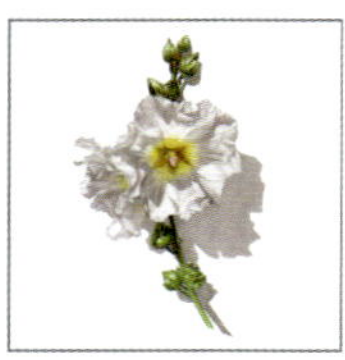

Page 7, 'Shelter'
White hollyhock – *Alcea rosea* 'Alba'

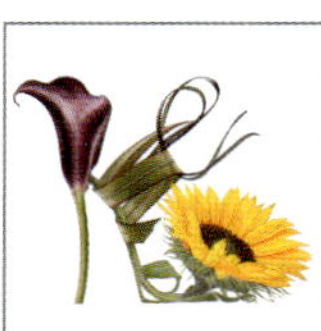

Page 24, 'Emma'
(Sunflower Shoe)
Sunflower – *Helianthus annuus*
Calla lily – *Zantedeschia* 'Cantor'
Flax – *Phormium tenax* 'Sundowner'
Black mondo grass – *Ophiopogon planiscapus*

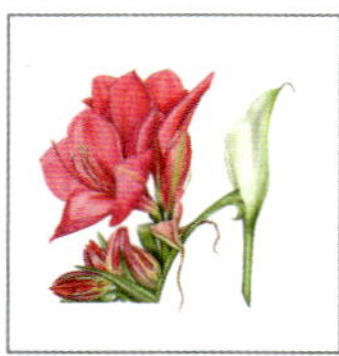

Page 8, 'Ionna' (Pink Shoe)
Hippeastrum 'Pink surprise'
White calla lily – *Zantedeschia aethiopica*
Tulipa 'Rococo'

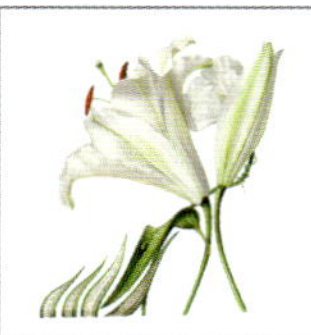

Page 25, 'Pura'
(White Lily Slipper)
Lilium regale 'Album'
Sweet pea – *Lathyrus latifolius* 'White Pearl'
Phormium 'Pink stripe'

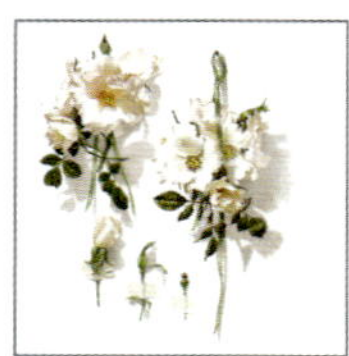

Page 11, 'White Star'
Rosa 'White Star'

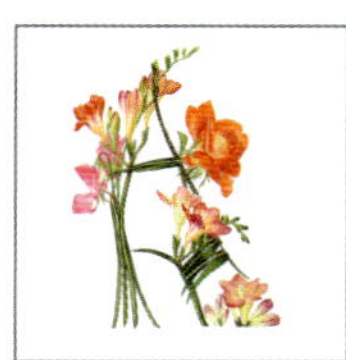

Pages 26 and 27, 'Odele'
(Sweet Orange Shoe)
Freesia 'Double Orange'
Hybrid tea rose – *Rosa* 'Jack's Wish'
Ribbon grass – *Phalaris arundinacea*
Sweet pea – *Lathyrus odoratus* 'Geranium Pink'

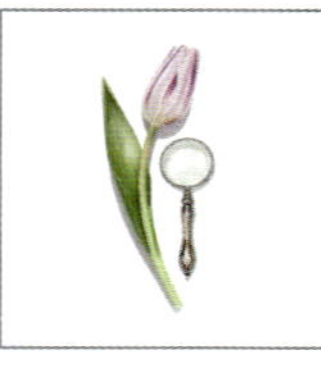

Page 12, 'Let's See'
(Tulip and Glass)
Tulipa 'Rems Favourite'

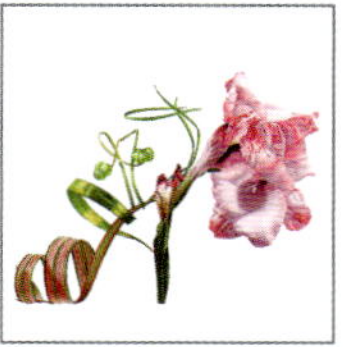

Page 29, 'Juliette'
(Gladioli Party Shoe)
Gladiolus 'Priscilla'
Phormium 'Pink Panther'
Nasturtium seeds
Blue fescue grass – *Festuca glauca*

PLANTS IN ORDER OF APPEARANCE

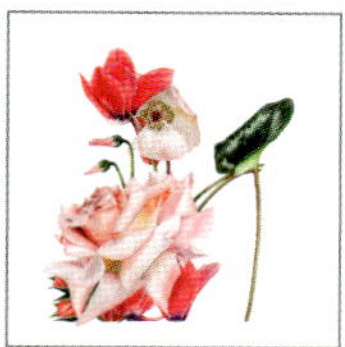

Pages 30 and 31, 'Isabella'
(Rose Slipper)
Paeonia lactiflora 'Sarah Bernhardt'
Cyclamen – *Cyclamen persicum*

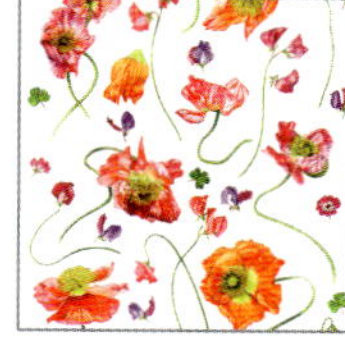

Page 42, 'Summer Pattern'
Icelandic poppy – *Papaver nudicaule*
Sweet pea – *Lathyrus sp.*
Leaf – *Geranium rotundifolium*
Alpine rose – *Rosa pendulina*

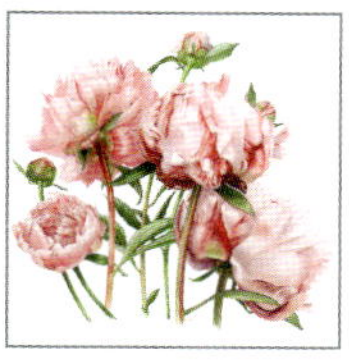

Page 32, 'Pink Summer'
Paeonia lactiflora 'Dinner Plate'
Paeonia lactiflora 'Sarah Bernhardt'

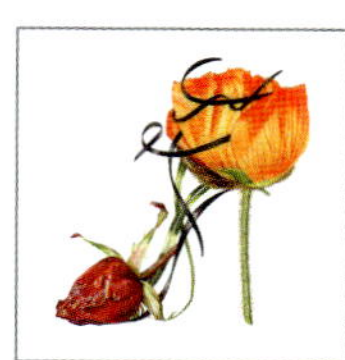

Page 44, 'Jessica'
(Orange Poppy Shoe)
Icelandic poppy – *Papaver nudicaule*
Rosa 'My Valentine' (straps)
Black mondo grass – *Ophiopogon planiscapus*
Grass – *Miscanthus sinensis* 'Strictus'

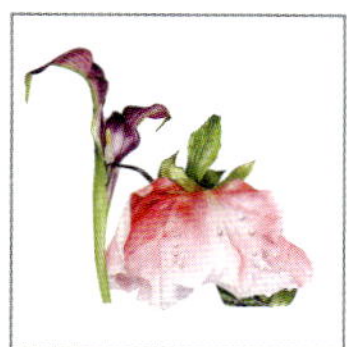

Page 33, 'Layla'
(Peony Slipper)
Paeonia × suffruticosa 'Hana Kisoi'
Zantedeschia 'Purple Heart'

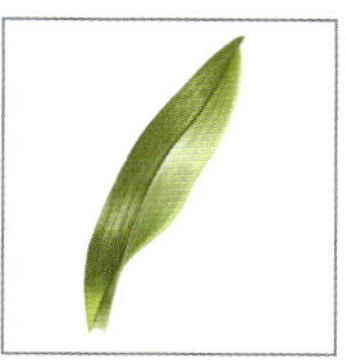

Pages 44 and 45, centre, orchid leaf

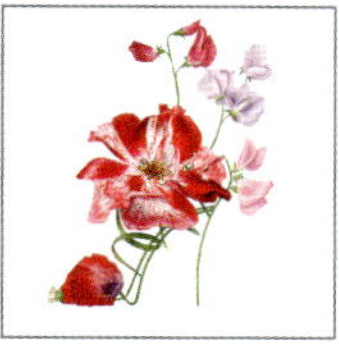

Pages 35 and 43, 'Scarlett'
(Sweet Crazy Shoe)
Sweet pea *Lathyrus latifolius*
Rosa gallica 'Versicolor'
Poppy – *Papaver somniferum*

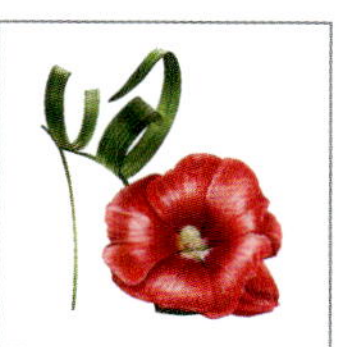

Page 45, 'Katya'
(Red Hollyhock Shoe)
Day lily leaf – *Hemerocallis*
Hollyhock – *Alcea* 'Henry III'

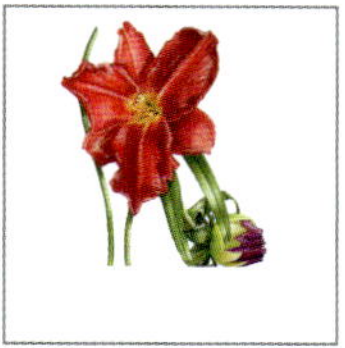

Pages 36 and 38, 'Jane'
(Day Lily Slipper)
Day lily – *Hemerocallis* 'Red Razzmatazz'
Dahlia 'Bacardi'

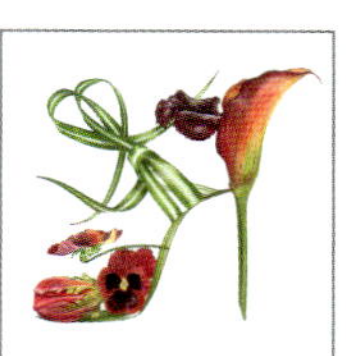

Pages 46 and 47, 'Laurie'
(Carnival Shoe)
Zantedeschia 'Fire Dancer'
Oshima sedge – *Carex hachijoensis* 'Evergold'
Tulipa 'Rococo'
Pansy – *Viola tricolor var.*

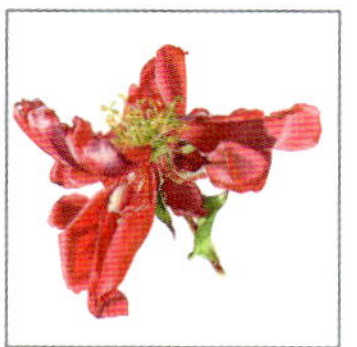

Page 39, 'Deep Pink Peony'
Paeonia lactiflora 'Karl Rosenfield'
See the tutorial at www.billyshowell.com

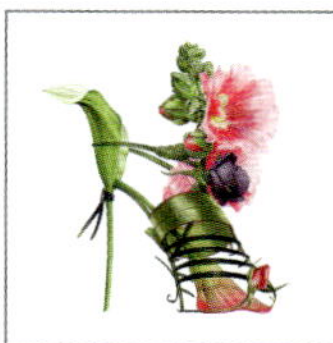

Pages 48 and 49, 'Holly'
(Pink Hollyhock Shoe)
Calla lily – *Zantedeschia*
Black mondo grass – *Ophiopogon planiscapus*
Phormium 'Red-Dark Green'
Helleborus 'Double Ellen Purple'
Pink hollyhock – *Alcea rosea*

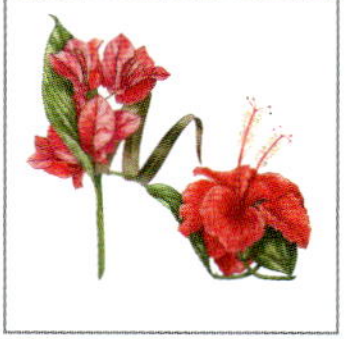

Page 40, 'Dorothy'
(Hibiscus Shoe)
Hibiscus rosa sinensis
Bougainvillea spectabilis
Leaf – *Epipremnum aureum*
Phormium tenax 'Purpureum'

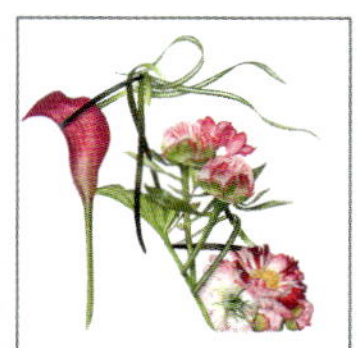

Page 51, 'Zoe'
(Peony Shoe)
Calla lily – *Zantedeschia* (straps)
Oshima sedge – *Carex hachijoensis* 'Evergold'
Black mondo grass – *Ophiopogon planiscapus*
Rosa gallica 'Versicolor', *Weigela florida* 'Purpurea'
Paeonia lactiflora 'Sarah Bernhardt'

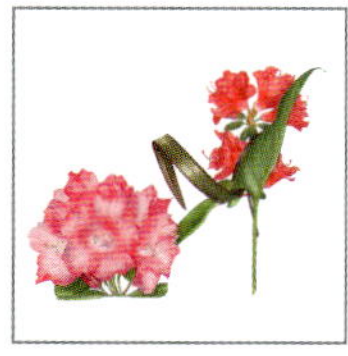

Page 41, 'Amelie'
(Pink Rhododendron shoe)
Calla lily leaf – *Zantedeschia* 'Green Goddess'
Azalea – *Rhododendron indicum*
Phormium 'Red-Dark Green'
Rhododendron ponticum 'Graziella'

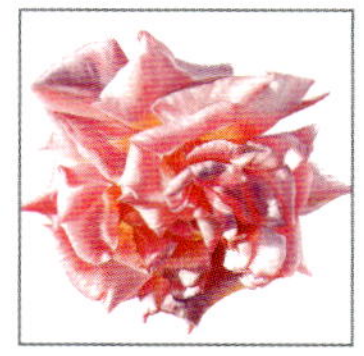

Page 52, 'Evening Pink Rose'
Hybrid tea – *Rosa* 'Compassion'

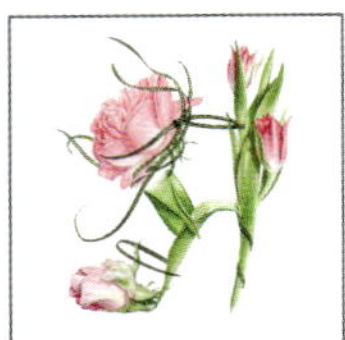

Page 54, 'Lucy'
(Pink Rose Shoe)
Rosa 'Bonica'
Tulipa 'Happy Family'
Leaves – *Miscanthus sinensis* 'Variegatus'

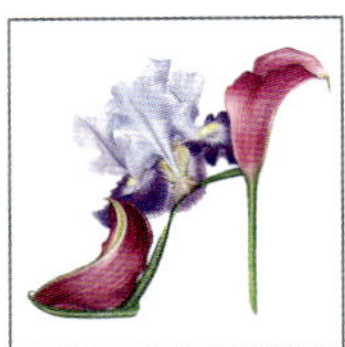

Page 66, 'Bella'
(Calla and Iris Shoe)
Zantedeschia 'Purple Sensation'
Iris germanica 'Emma Louise'

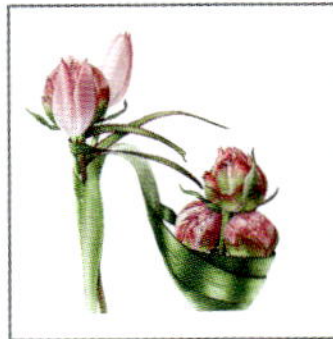

Page 55, 'Arianna'
(Party Shoe)
Paeonia lactiflora 'Sarah Bernhardt'
Tulipa 'Pink Diamond'
Juvenile *Phormium* leaves

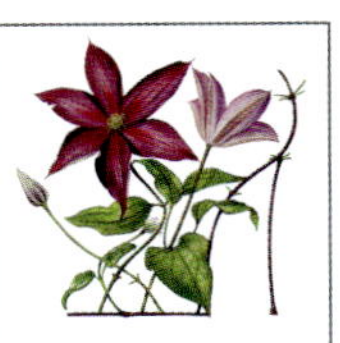

Page 68, 'Florence'
(Clematis Sandal)
Clematis 'The Vagabond'

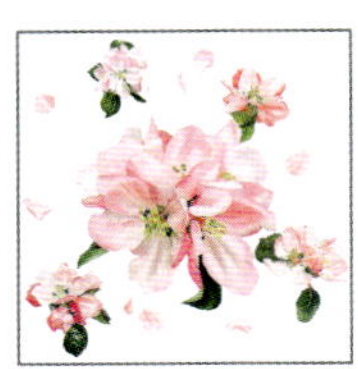

Page 56, 'Apple blossom'
Malus 'Bramley's Seedling'

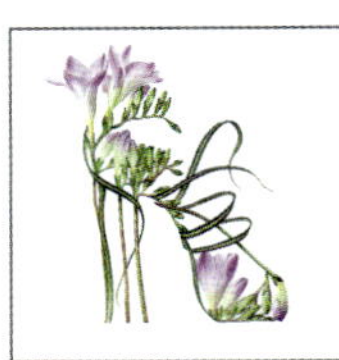

Page 69, 'Alice'
(Freesia Sandal)
Lilac-coloured freesia

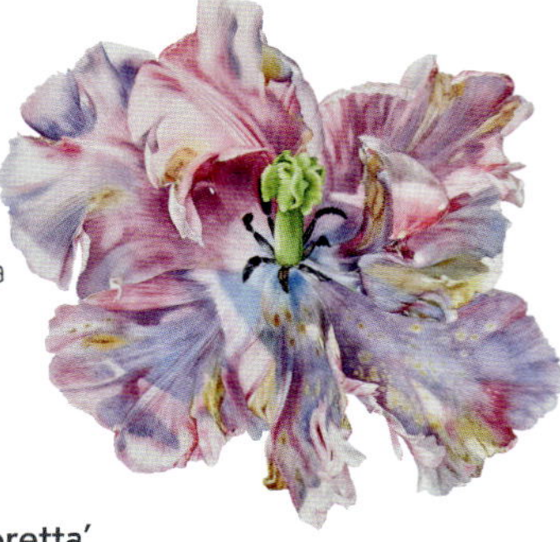

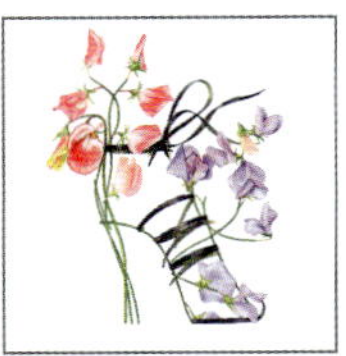

Pages 70 and 71, 'Loretta'
(Sweet Pea Sandal)
Sweet pea – *Lathyrus odoratus* (heel, toe
and decoration)
Black mondo grass – *Ophiopogon
planiscapus* (straps)

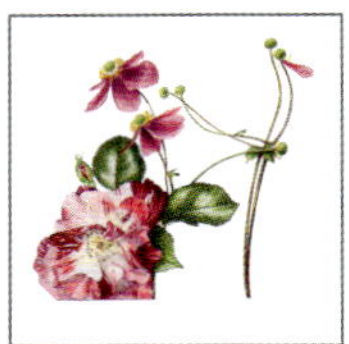

Page 57, 'Elizabeth'
(Black Calla and Pink Rose Shoe)
Rosa 'Bonica'
Black mondo grass – *Ophiopogon planiscapus*
Arum lily – *Zantedeschia* 'Schwarzwalder'
Zantedeschia 'Black Forest'

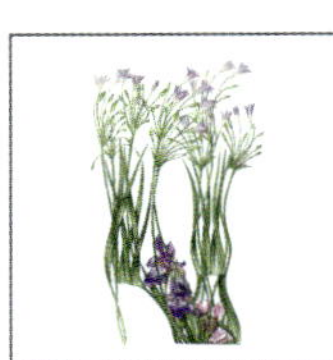

Page 72, 'Breya'
(Iris Boot)
Iris – *Iris sibirica*
French lavender – *Lavandula stoechas*
Triteleia laxa 'Ithuriel's Spear'

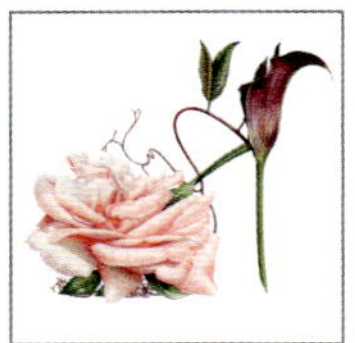

Pages 58 and 59, 'Millie'
(Crazy for You Rose Slipper)
Rosa 'Crazy for You'
Anemone hupehensis 'Jasmine'

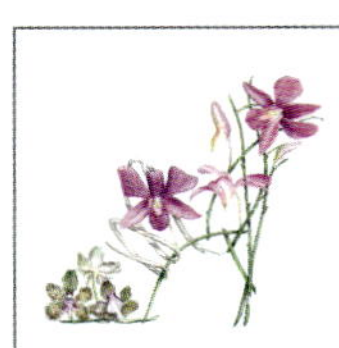

Page 73, 'Delphina'
(Orchid Shoe)
Orchidaceae Vanda tessellate
Orchidaceae Dendrobium 'Sampran Brown'

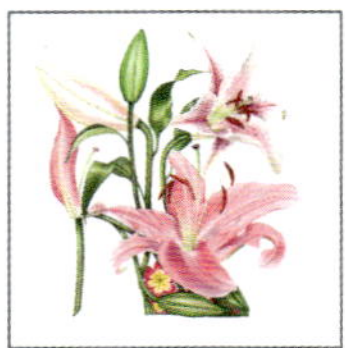

Pages 60 and 61, 'Eva'
(New Pink Rose Slipper)
Rosa 'Communis'
Zantedeschia 'Akela' (straps)
Alpine *Clematis* leaves and tendrils

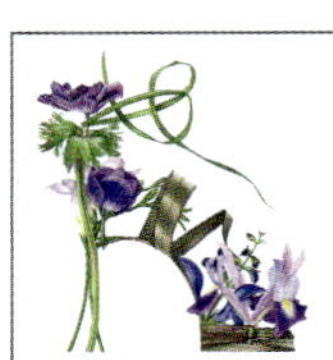

Pages 74 and 75, 'Brontë'
(Blue Evening Shoe)
Purple *Anemone coronaria*
Lilac-coloured *Freesia*
Phormium 'Red-Dark Green'
Salvia guaranitica 'Black and Blue'
Iris sibirica (hybrid unknown)

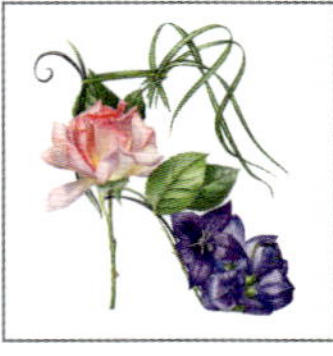

Page 62, 'Rita'
(Pink Lily Shoe)
Lilium 'Stargazer'
Lilium L.A. hybrid
Primula

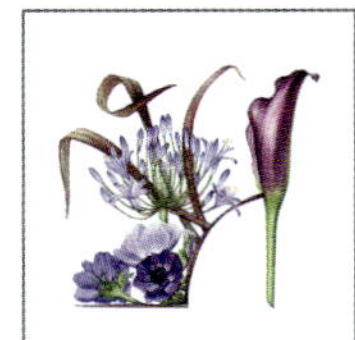

Page 78, 'Aphrodite'
(Blue Shoe)
Calla lily – *Zantedeschia* 'Akela',
Purple *Anemone coronaria*
Agapanthus 'Brilliant Blue'
Flax *Phormium tenax* 'Purpureum'

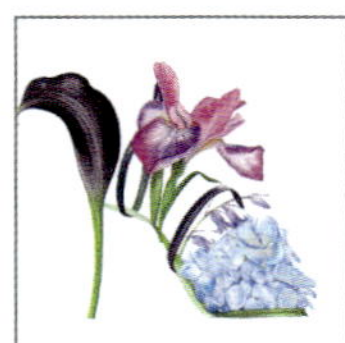

Page 64, 'Margot'
(Violet and Rose Shoe)
Balloon flower – *Platycodon grandifloras*
Rosa 'Bonica'
Oshima sedge – *Carex hachijoensis* 'Evergold'

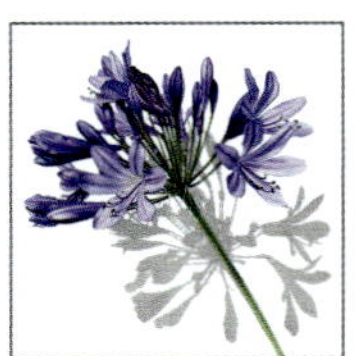

Page 79
Agapanthus 'Margaret'

Page 65, 'Harmony'
(Late Summer Slipper)
Calla lily – *Zantedeschia* 'Cantor'
Hydrangea macrophylla 'Little Blue'
Black mondo grass – *Ophiopogon planiscapus*
Iris sibirica 'Sparkling Rose'

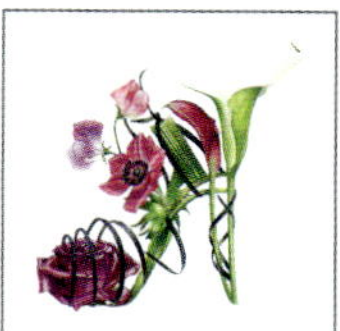

Pages 80 and 81, 'Anastasia'
(Caged Love)
Calla lily – *Zantedeschia*
Floribunda rose – *Rosa* 'Ebb Tide'
Black mondo grass – *Ophiopogon planiscapus*
Sweet pea – *Lathyrus odoratus*
Anemone – *Anemone coronaria*

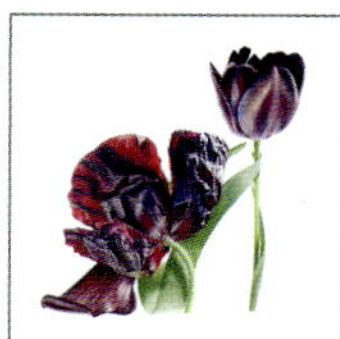

Pages 82 and 83, 'Hesper'
(Black Party Shoe)
Tulipa 'Queen of Night'
Zantedeschia 'Be My Heart'
Papaver somniferum 'Black Single'
Tulipa leaf

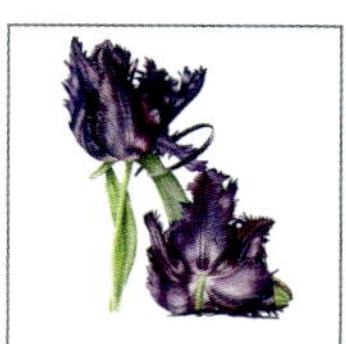

Pages 86 and 87, 'Luna'
(Tulip Night Shoe)
Tulipa 'Black Parrot'

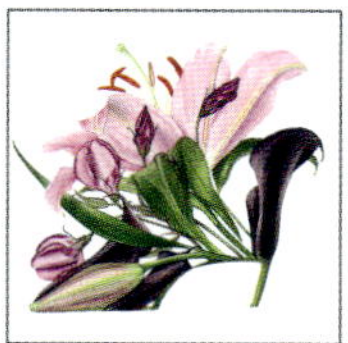

Pages 88 and 89, 'Ursula'
(Black Evening Slipper)
Black calla lily – *Zantedeschia* 'Cantor'
Lily L.A. hybrid
Variagated lisianthus – *Eustoma grandiflorum*

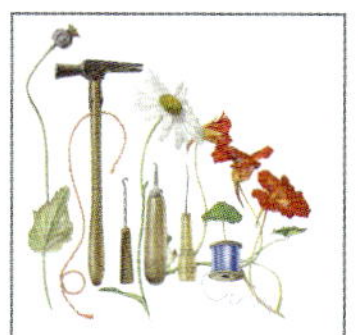

Page 91, 'The Shoemaker's Tools'
Left to right:
Poppy seed head – *Papava somniferum*
Oxeye daisy – *Leucanthemum vulgare*
Nasturtium – *Tropaeolum majus*

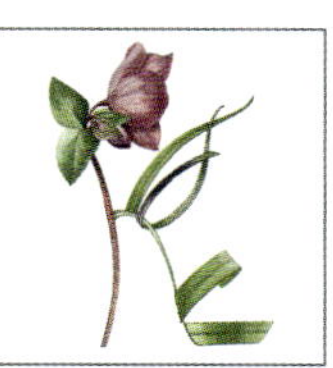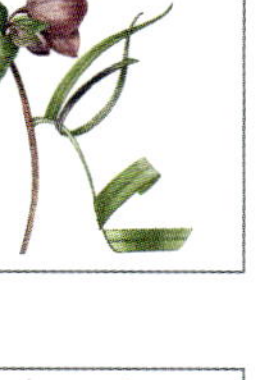

Page 92, 'Aiyanna'
(Hellebore Sandal)
Helleborus 'Penny's Pink'
Day lily leaves
Black mondo grass – *Ophiopogon planiscapus*
Oshima sedge – *Carex hachijoensis* 'Evergold'

Page 94, 'Ophelia'
(Tulip Boot)
Tulipa 'Angelique'

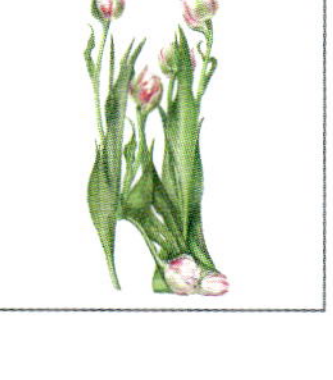

Page 96, 'Queenie'
(Green Queen)
Tulipa 'White rebel'
Phormium 'Red-Dark Green'

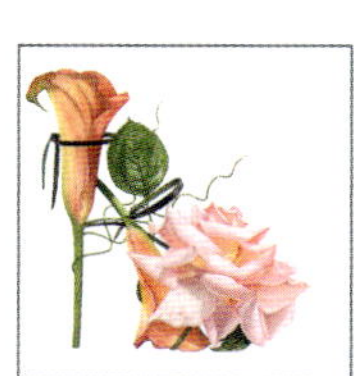

Page 98, 'Edith'
(Summer Joy Rose Shoe)
Zantedeschia 'Captain Amigo'
Black mondo grass – *Ophiopogon planiscapus*
Rosa 'Compassion'
Corkscrew rush – *Juncus effusus f. spiralis*

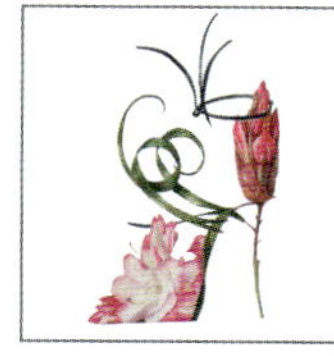

Page 99, 'Linda'
(Linda's Shoe)
Rhododendron 'Bow Bells'
Day lily leaves
Black mondo grass – *Ophiopogon planiscapus*

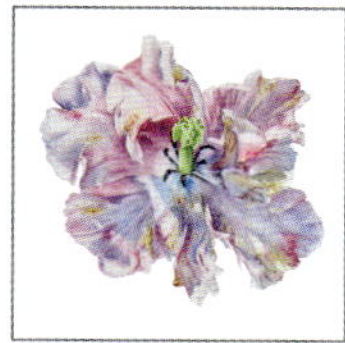

Opposite and below, 'Crazy Tulip'
Tulipa 'Blue Parrot'

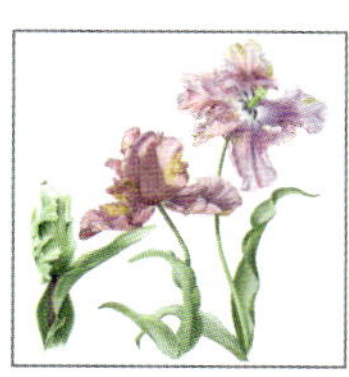

Page 104, 'Crazy Tulips'
Tulipa 'Blue Parrot'
Tulipa 'Green Wave'

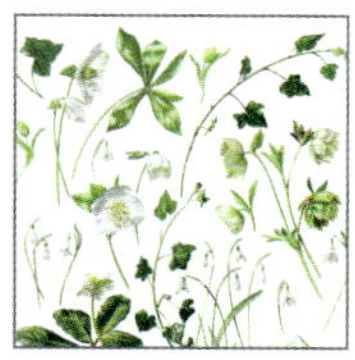

Inside back endpapers, 'Winter Pattern'
Christmas rose – *Helleborus niger*
Snowdrop – *Galanthus nivalis*
Common ivy – *Hedera helix*
Helleborus 'Double Ellen Green'

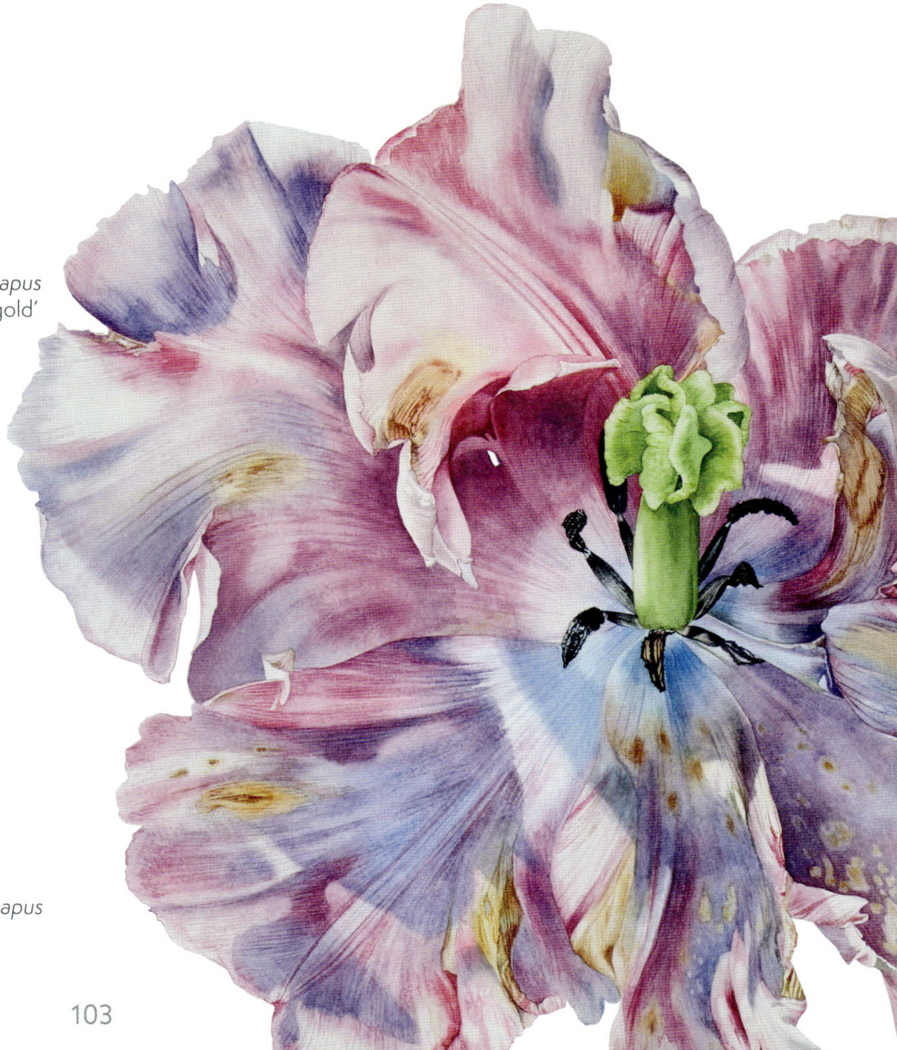

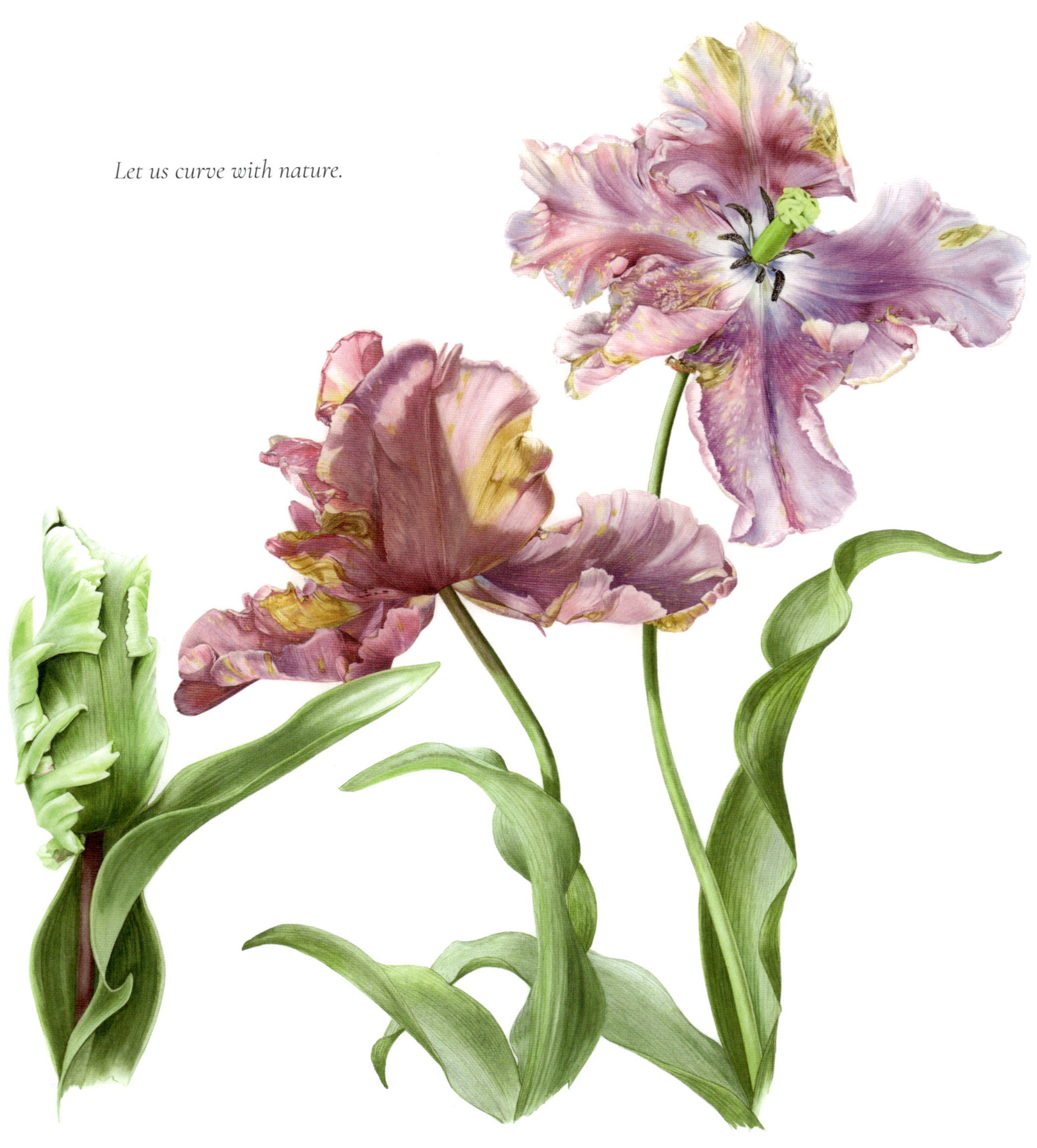

Let us curve with nature.

In winter cold, I look for signs
Of green shoots pushing through,
From deep beneath the rich, dark soil
To wave beneath sky blue.
To grow and reach to be admired
And curve in the shape of the shoe.
To walk us to the garden
I chose to walk with you.

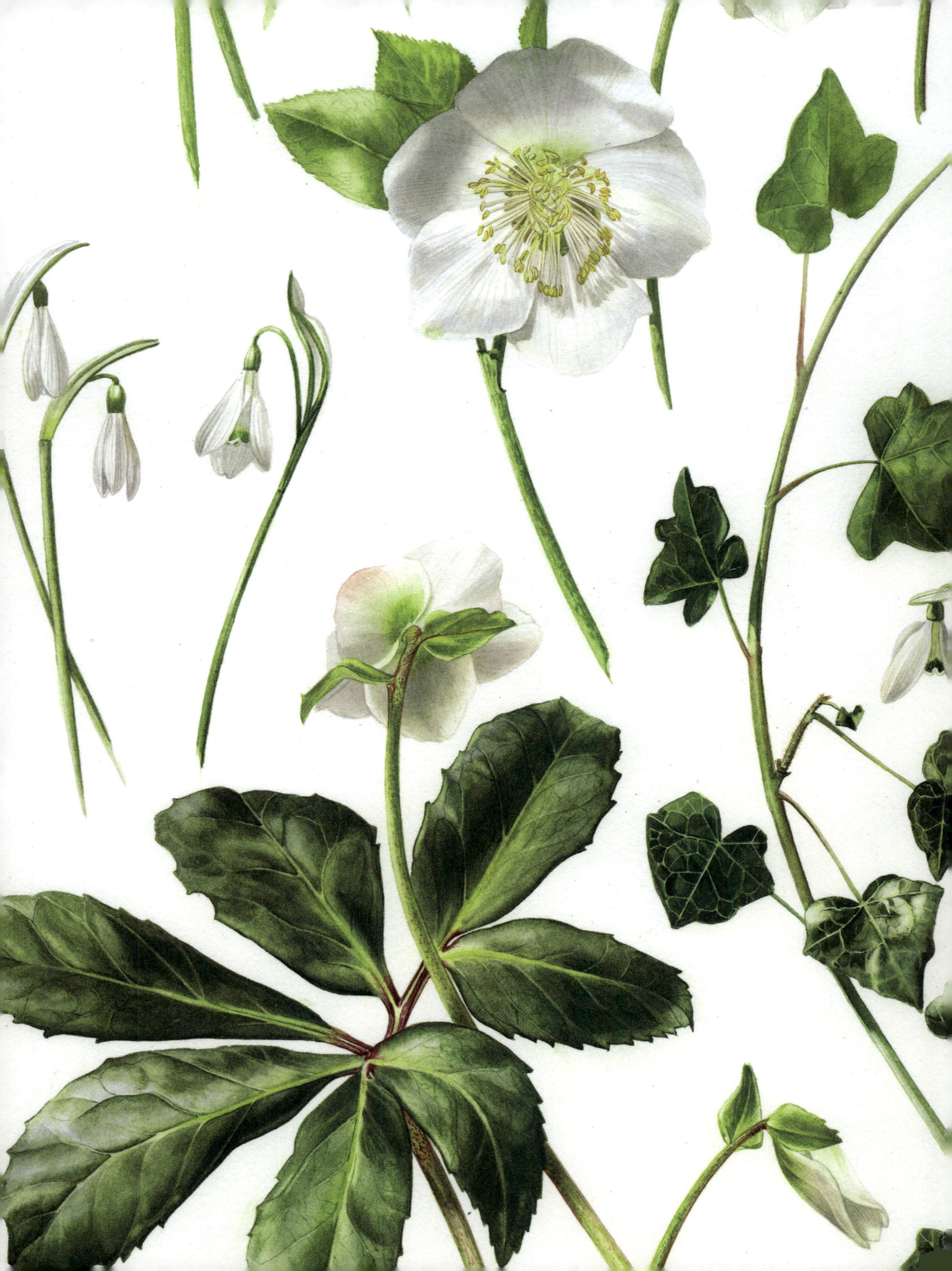